42454

The Last Victorian

The Last Victorian

R. D. Blackmore and his novels

by

KENNETH BUDD

LONDON
CENTAUR PRESS
1960

First published 1960 by Centaur Press Ltd., 9 St. Anne's Close, London, N.6, and printed in Great Britain by T. J. Winterson, London, in 11 on 13pt. Baskerville

FOR BETTY
WITH LOVE

Illustrations

Foreword

In his autobiography *From the Angle of 88*, Mr. Eden Philpotts (to whom Blackmore gave early encouragement) has said that he could not remember "any searching valuation of Blackmore's work as an artist." "I always feel that Blackmore has lacked of the homage his achievement demanded." Since those words were written (in 1951), Professor Waldo Dunn, of Scripps College, Claremont, California, has published (1956) his biography of R. D. Blackmore, which is likely to be definitive. The book, penned (as its author would agree) "this side idolatry", concentrates on the facts of its subject's life rather than on his works. It is the purpose of the present study to combine an outline biography with some comments on the novels, in the hope that modern readers may be led to discover and appreciate the several excellent books that have languished for too long in the shade of *Lorna Doone*.

My chief thanks are due to Professor Dunn himself for his generous encouragement and valuable suggestions. Other scholars in the United States have been notable examples of that American cordiality which Blackmore himself experienced. Thanks are also expressed to the Trustees of the British Museum Library, to Mr. John Butler, to Mr. J. Alex Symington, to Messrs. Rockliff for permission to quote extracts from *Poor Monkey* by Peter Coveney, and to Peter Owen for a quotation from *The Development of the Detective Novel*, by A. E. Murch, and to Messrs. Jonathan Cape for an extract from *Some Victorian Wallflowers*, by Malcolm Elwin.

K.G.B.

I

LONGWORTH, a village of some eight hundred inhabitants, in the county of Berkshire, is situated in the pleasant country of the White Horse. It lies below Harrowdown Hill, on the very edge of the Oxfordshire border, and is a little over a mile from the southern bank of the Thames at this point; Oxford is ten miles away to the north-east. Walkers and ramblers who want to see something of the sequestered villages beneath the Berkshire Downs are likely to confine themselves to the Streatley and Wantage area, or to explore the neighbourhood of Uffington ; those who feel that they might like to have a look at Longworth will probably do so on account of its Norman and Decorated church. They will be unaware that it is the birthplace of two men, separated by two hundred years, whose immortality rests in the one case on the authorship of a single novel, and in the other on being the subject of an epigram. The first is R. D. Blackmore and the second is Dr. John Fell, and both could claim with justification that they had been in this way most unfairly treated by posterity. *Lorna Doone* was not the only considerable achievement of its writer, and Dr. Fell's eminence as an architect, and his wide influence on the Oxford of his time, have counted little in human memory beside the fact that he was once the victim of a student's ready wit. "I do not like thee, Dr. Fell," is in every book of quotations.

The reader of *Lorna Doone* who notes the lengthy

11

and detailed description, in the sixty-ninth chapter, of the coat of arms awarded by the King to Sir John Ridd, will not be surprised to learn that its author had a life-long interest in heraldry, and once favoured a friend with an account of his own armorial bearings:

> "The three chevrons, in my arms are gules, and the pales, or pallets, are red, too, supposed to indicate bloody strokes (by a royal hand) upon the shield of one of my ancestors, who fought well."

In the same letter he included a reference to his ancestry:

> "My father's forbears were North Devon yeomen, and small landowners for three years at Parracombe; but my mother's were of blue blood."

Neither of the yeomen nor of the blue blood, however, is there a great deal that can be set down with certainty. In local registers the Blackmore pedigree can be traced back to the John Blackmore of Parracombe, who died in 1689. A hundred years or so later another John Blackmore emerged from his farming background, went up to Exeter College, Oxford, and after ordination became curate of High Bray, on the outskirts of Exmoor. While there he bought the advowson of the adjacent living of Charles, hoping that he might shortly present himself as the Rector. West country clergy, however, are noted for longevity, and when over fifty years had passed before the vacancy occurred, the patron felt himself to be too old to fill it. In the interim he had become Rector of Oare and of Combe Martin, and he held these in plurality for nine years.

His two sons, John and Richard, both took Holy Orders, and when the parish of Charles at last was available, he presented it to the younger. There is no information as to why the elder was passed over; possibly the patron reckoned that the latter's high classical attainments and strong force of character might make him less dependent on paternal privileges. Unfortunately the choice was the wrong one, and a legend persisted in family circles that the parsonage at Charles was ever afterwards haunted by the repentant spirit of the father bewailing his unjust selection. In 1822 John Blackmore married Anne Basset, the eldest daughter of a former Vicar of Tewkesbury, himself descended from a wealthy merchant who was twice Mayor of Bristol. These two were the novelist's parents.

When Richard Doddridge Blackmore was born, on June 7, 1825, his father was a coach for Oxford students, the proximity of Longworth to the University being the chief reason for his choice of it as a place of residence. He also held the curacy of Culmstock, near Wellington, in Somerset; a distance of a hundred miles or so between a parson and his people not being considered in those days any disqualification for the receipt of the stipend from the parish thus "served".[1] The child was given the second name of Doddridge in admiring memory of the

---

[1] An Act of 1803 had, often unsuccessfully, ordered the clergy to reside in their parishes.

13

robust and distinctly broad-minded divine of the eighteenth century, who was a great-grandfather of R. D. Blackmore on his maternal side. So were linked the genial Free Churchman and the staunch Anglican, and although Blackmore had no special love for "dissenters" he was quite happy to bear the name of a man whom he regarded as a good and eminently sensible Christian.

The tranquil story of yeomen and parsons in the combes and meadows of a world that seems across the years to be a Paradise from which humanity would never be turned out, is suddenly shadowed by one of those strokes of evil which man acknowledges in the scheme of things, but for which he is never personally prepared. Richard Doddridge was only three months old when an outbreak of typhus in the village struck terribly at the Blackmore household, carrying off John's wife and all the servants, with the family physician himself a victim. Fifty years later, when he was writing *Cripps the Carrier,* set in the neighbourhood of Oxford, Blackmore, with this personal tragedy in mind, permitted himself one of the few autobiographical echoes, and one of the many reflections on human nature and conduct, that appear in his novels :

"This was the time to show what stuff both men and women were made of. Fair-weather visitors, and delightful gossips, and the most devoted friends, stood far aloof from the tainted gale, and fumigated their letters. The best of them sent their grooms to the lodge, with orders to be very careful, and to be sure to use tobacco during the moment of colloquy.

Others had so much faith that everything would be ordered for the best, that they went to the seaside at once, to be delivered from presumption. Many saw a visitation for some secret sin, that otherwise might have festered inwardly and destroyed the immortal part . . .

Leaving these to go their way, a few kind souls came fluttering to the house of pestilence and death. Two housemaids, and the boy who cleaned the servants' shoes, had been struck down, and never rose again, except with very cautious liftings into their last narrow cells. The disease had spread from their master; and their constitutions were not like his. Also the senior footman and the under-cook, were in their beds; but the people who had their work to do believed them to be only shamming."

The catastrophe also carried off Blackmore's only sister in her infancy, but a brother, Henry John, born a year before Richard, survived it, to die fifty years later in somewhat mysterious circumstances at Yeovil. Of this elder brother scarcely anything is known but his local reputation for eccentricity and his fondness for scientific experiments, and not one of the accounts of him that have been left can be reckoned to his credit.

Something of a West Country mist has closed over Blackmore's early boyhood. No one, as far as is known, has preserved any reminiscences of him at that time which might have thrown interesting light on his developing character, and he himself has left no record of his childhood ambitions, tastes and follies. Some years after the Longworth tragedy, John Blackmore married again, and the boy subsequently spent many of his vacations at his uncle's home in the moorland village of Charles or with his uncle in Glamorganshire. Nearly thirty years after the publication of *Lorna Doone* Blackmore produced a collection of short stories with the same setting, and in the Preface he allows us a glimpse of the ancient Parsonage at Charles, "where the lawn is a russet sponge of moss, and a stream trickles under the dining-room floor," and of himself as a boy amidst the scenes and silences of a place as remote from the highways of men as any in the whole of England at that time :

> "Sometimes of a night, when the spirit of a dream flits away for a waltz with the shadow of a pen, over dreary moors and dark waters, I behold an old man, with a keen profile, under a parson's shovel hat, riding a tall chestnut horse up the western slope of Exmoor, followed by his little grandson upon a shaggy and stuggy pony."

Sir Herbert Warren (for some years President of Magdalen College, Oxford) who came to know Blackmore well enough to visit him on several occasions and to exchange with him many friendly letters, stated in his Introduction to the "World's Classics" edition (1914) of *Lorna Doone* that Blackmore's first school was at Bruton, in Somerset. He also remarked, quoting someone unknown, that Blackmore at the age of five was accustomed to take the "Edinburgh Review" to read in bed—the sort of biographical fragment which its subject, who warmly disliked priggishness and precocity, would have

R. D. BLACKMORE

preferred to remain untold. The statement about Bruton was confirmed by Professor Waldo Dunn,[1] who discovered a letter written by Blackmore at the age of nine and showing beyond question that he was then a scholar at the King's School in that little town. It had replaced, in the reign of Edward VI, an earlier school founded in 1519 and swept away, along with the Abbey, at the Dissolution. "I do not," said the little boy, "like it at all."

The mist comes down again over the childish sadnesses and achings of the next three years, but divides again on an August day in 1837 to disclose Blackmore entering the gates of Blundell's School at Tiverton in Devon. The building at that time was on the bank of the Lowman stream, about a mile from the position of the present school, and the number of boys in the Upper and Lower Schools combined did not reach a hundred and fifty. In that small world, in which fighting, drinking, and bullying were the accompaniments of the sound classical education desired for young gentlemen by Mr. Peter Blundell, clothier, a small boy could suffer much, and there is no doubt that Blackmore had his times of mental and physical pain during the next six years. One who knew him later declared that the retrospect of the misery and privations of his boyhood affected him to his closing days with a lively sense of horror and disgust. The opening chapters of *Lorna Doone* seem to indicate that the statement is an exaggeration, and we have for guidance in the matter only the fact of Blackmore's sensitive

[1] *R. D. Blackmore.*

17

B

nature and the reputation of the school in those years for roughness and toughness.

Blackmore shared lodgings with Frederick and John Temple, who had entered the school three years and two years earlier respectively, in Cops Court, so-called from one of the school porters. There they lived very economically, the fees for town boys at that time being about £4 a year. Frederick Temple does not appear to have been a particularly kindly or gentle sponsor, and Blackmore has nowhere acknowledged any special indebtedness to the future Archbishop of Canterbury. Temple had, of course, moral and spiritual qualities of a high order, but he was not always sensitive to other people's feelings, and there are stories of him which reveal a harsh side to his character. He could hold his own in a rough-and-tumble more effectively than his reserved fellow-pupil, and many years afterwards when he visited the "ironing-box" (the triangular patch of grass at Blundell's where fights took place) he referred in an enthusiastic manner to his first victory on that spot and to the combats he subsequently enjoyed. The "just beast", bearing one of the most venerated names in the modern history of the Church of England, has received from many angles an ample measure of praise; but there are some others who glimpsed those weaknesses in a mighty man which contributed to Blackmore's periods of unhappiness as a schoolboy. One who was a pupil of Temple's when he later was Principal of the Kneller Hall Training College for Teachers at Twickenham, afterwards wrote in a letter to a friend: "I am indisposed to believe that Mr. Temple was by nature a kind-hearted man. My own theory . . . is that he compelled himself to do the many kindly actions which indicated sympathy. It seemed to me, and still seems, that there were two spirits striving within him for mastery, a naturally domineering spirit, and a determination to act in a just and kindly manner." The evil spirit appears sometimes to have been the victor in Temple's relations with his fag, and F. J. Snell (the historian of Blundell's) declares that the attacks of epilepsy to which Blackmore was subject for some years after this period were caused largely by ill-treatment.

In spite of such troubles, however, Blackmore's natural ability asserted itself. He achieved some eminence as a classical scholar, became head boy for two years, and obtained the Giffard scholarship to Exeter College, Oxford, where he matriculated on December 7, 1843.

Blackmore crossed this threshold in the dawning hour of his country's entry upon an age of material prosperity which he, like so many of his contemporaries, regarded as a sure sign of Divine favour, and he did not live to see any serious threat to that immensely satisfying stability. In that year the traveller from London could get as far as Folkestone by rail for the first time, British exports were going in rapidly increasingly quantities to every corner of the earth, and income tax was at sevenpence in the pound. In the literary world *Martin Chuzzlewit* was appearing in monthly numbers, Lord Lytton's novels were selling enormously, and multitudes were reading the works of Sir Walter Scott and Fenimore Cooper in

Bentley's and Colburn's "Standard Novels." In Dorchester, William Barnes, singing of the beauty of wedded love and midsummer meadows with the passion with which Blackmore was later to extol them in prose, was preparing for publication his *Poems of Rural Life in the Dorset Dialect*.

In Blackmore's Oxford the chief topics of conversation in the intervals between running into debt, hunting, ragging, rowing, and going to lectures, were Apostolic Succession, the Thirty-Nine Articles of Religion, and the various doctrinal issues that had been raised by Newman, Pusey and Keble. Beyond the dreaming spires Chartist agitators were engaged in the more important battles of their own. Of the whole population of England over 40% was illiterate, and the nation had a million and a half paupers. The only form of recreation open to the working-class was alcohol. The Bolton Report had given a picture of those who, in "the hungry forties," were outside the benefits of the rising tide of economic prosperity. "Anything like the squalid misery," it said, "the slow, mouldering, putrefying death by which the weak and feeble of the working classes are perishing here, it never befell eyes to behold nor imagination to conceive . . . Men, women, and children pent up in a dusty atmosphere from five in the morning till seven at night, without change, without intermission, from week to week, fled to the beer-shops on Saturday nights to forget their misery. In such towns few of the labouring classes lived to be thirty: you might occasionally see tottering and broken men and women, grey-haired and aged, whom you took to be eighty, but who were in fact thirty-five or forty." At a meeting in Leeds at the end of 1841, it was shown that there were nearly twenty thousand individuals in the city with only 11¼d. a week per head to live on. In the age of paradox they were building the Royal yacht, "Victoria and Albert," at Pembroke, and in the Fleet Prison, shortly to be closed, there was a debtor who had been confined in it for his offence for over thirty years!

At Oxford Blackmore no doubt made his opinions emphatically known on the subject of "ritualism"; the "downright, ordinary Englishman" who was suspicious of the Tractarians and the introduction of "Popish cere-monies," and even of the revival of monastic life as a result of the Oxford Movement, had all his sympathy. He had little patience with those who wanted the Church of England to be other than as he had always known it; he had been reared in an atmosphere of what would be called to-day "Low Church" Protestantism, with "sen-sible" services, and he was never prepared to move an inch from this position. More than half a century later he made, in a letter to a friend, a scornful reference to a local church as being "conducted on the Marinette and Popinjay system, now so fashionable here, which I look upon as a weak sham of papistry."

But there were better and brighter things for his atten-tion than these ecclesiastical controversies. He had chess and angling for his leisure hours, and all around him with their Virgilian delights were the

"wide grass meadows which the sunshine fills."

21

They came to mean to him, at least in retrospect, what they meant to Matthew Arnold, who was later to reveal his determined "Oxonolatry," and who was, in the closing days of Blackmore's time at Exeter, about to be elected to a Fellowship at Oriel.

II

THE year 1847, during which Blackmore came down from Oxford with second-class honours in Classics, brought him a happiness that became the real inspiration of his life and strongly affected his manipulation of the lives of those many young lovers whom he delighted to create. While he was with a reading-party at St. Helier, in Jersey, he met an Irish girl named Lucy Maguire. We know nothing of her appearance, and the fact that Blackmore certainly modelled the qualities and characteristics of a number of his fictional heroines upon those he extolled in Lucy gives us scarcely anything of a portrait. He was never able, or never cared, to clothe his characters in such well-defined material form that their features are as clear to us as their vices or virtues. In *Kit and Kitty*, Blackmore has devoted a paragraph to a description of Kitty Fairthorn which is typical of his somewhat cursory manner of attempting a picture of the heroine; and this may well contain some reminiscence of his own sweetheart as he had seen her in earlier years :

"She wore a grey cloak looking wonderfully simple, yet gathered in small at her beautiful waist, and trimmed at the skirts, and over two little pockets, with a soft blue fur called Vicunha. And she carried a little muff of the same material, and the strings of her hat (which was like a sea-shell) were also of a blue tint very sweetly matching. But the blue that was sweetest and richest of all was that of her large, soft, loving eyes, than which it is impossible for any poet to imagine anything in heaven more lovely."

It happened that Lucy Maguire was a Roman Catholic, and one is tempted to speculate on what would have befallen them both if she had remained as antagonistic to Blackmore's denominational outlook as he was to hers. But the course of their true love was not halted by this situation, and Blackmore never had to decide between the desires of his heart and the dictates of his reason. Lucy became an Anglican before the two were married in 1852, and ever afterwards shared his churchgoing as she shared in every triumph and sorrow of the thirty-six years they were to spend together.

Blackmore needed Lucy and those glimpses of heaven through her large and loving eyes, during the next few years; for it is certain that there were few other links with celestial blessedness in the surroundings in which he now spent his time. He had been entered as a member of the Middle Temple in 1845 and was now studying under one John Warner of the Inner Temple and Chancery Bar. He probably took Lucy to the Great Exhibition several times in order that she might be in no doubt as to the inevitability of the stupendous progress which the country had before it, taught her to play chess, and often amused her with his realistic descriptions of what went on amongst the legal masters and pupils. That Blackmore saw some humorous aspects in the sombre scene is amply testified in the early chapters of *Alice*

Lorraine, which are undoubtedly based on his own recollections of his training for the Law.

On June 7th in the year of his marriage, Blackmore was called to the Bar, his Chambers being at No. 3, Essex Court. That Blackmore should ever have seriously contemplated the Law as a life-long profession is surprising, in view of what we know of his tastes and talents. If his mother had not died in his infancy, he would probably have been influenced by her in an entirely different direction. But as a married man of twenty-seven, it was imperative for him to take up a lucrative post, and *Christowell* shows that he found some pleasant masters and colleagues during this period. The novel gives considerable prominence to a certain Mr. Latimer ("of the reputable firm of Latimer and Emblin"), and about the firm itself Blackmore makes the sort of amused and tolerant observation of particular human weaknesses that is found so often in Dickens:

"Messrs. Latimer & Emblin, of No. 10, Jackdaw's Court, Gray's Inn, had been in practice (through their ancestors, or selves), for upwards of a century; and their practice was quiet, and wise, and solid. With litigation they dealt so little, that if any one asked them who was the present Attorney-General, they went to the legal almanac to look, and after much consultation, sometimes put the saddle upon the wrong animal. Yet, being always accurate in the end, and very particular not to mislead, whenever they made a mistake, they always corrected it by post at a nominal charge. And if, while alive, any lawyer can conciliate affection, it is by acknowledging

25

that he was wrong; with a lenient charge for confessing it."

S. M. Ellis, who came to know Blackmore during the last six years or so of the novelist's life, and gathered a certain amount of information about him for a book on some Victorian writers, says that because of his susceptibility to epileptic seizures Blackmore could never appear in Court and so was compelled to relinquish office work and to turn to the more open-air life of an assistant schoolmaster. There are, however, obvious drawbacks even in that sort of career for one so afflicted, and Blackmore probably had other reasons for abandoning his legal practice. He did in fact become less liable to these distressing attacks in the years that followed, and the turning-point he had now reached led him within a short time to the place and the opportunity of which people of his talent and temperament so often dream and so rarely discover.

Blackmore applied for, and obtained, a post as classics master at Wellesley House School, on the main road from Twickenham to Hampton Court. The great rectangle of a house, with a flight of steps to double doors giving entrance to a hall of tunnel-like length and darkness, with a front garden shrouded in the towering shrubs beloved of the Victorians, might have given to some visitors a hint of the sinister activities within Dotheboys Hall. In fact, however, Blackmore was happy there and became so attached to the Headmaster, named Scalé, that he kept up the friendship for many years and in

1866 dedicated his novel *Cradock Nowell* to the latter's
memory. The school holidays gave Blackmore leisure
for walking, reading, and writing, and the fruit of the
last appeared in 1854 in *Poems by Melanter,* published
by Robert Hardwicke in London at 38 Carey Street. Like
Meredith and Hardy, Blackmore thus began his literary
career with the publication of poetry. The contents, both
of this little book and of a second collection of poems,
called *Epullia,* published later in the same year, indicate
the dominant interests of his life—the power and glory
of England (achieved, as he sincerely felt, by the God-
blessed standards and codes of the English gentleman),
and the rural scene. He later included a revised version
of one of these early poems ("A Harvest Song") in *Lorna
Doone.*

Blackmore had not to go far from the school to find
inspiration for a song of green fields, for this part of the
Thames Valley was then a region of trees, country lanes,
and splendid mansions in large grounds. The neighbourhood had indeed changed very little since the day, a
hundred years earlier, when Horace Walpole had
acquired his "little playing-house" at Strawberry Hill,
"set in enamelled meadows, with filigree hedges." Blackmore and his wife lived within a hundred yards of the
river which had been close to him in its upper reaches
during his childhood. They occupied a square, Georgian
dwelling in a quiet road running between Teddington
Lock and Hampton Wick, and Blackmore christened it
"Gomer House", which name it has continued to bear
through a century of changes that have erased almost

everything else of the village he knew. The time was a happy one for the man who was free now from the loneliness of his boyhood and the dullness of legal documents, and could rejoice in his love, in the pleasures of a little garden and the sunlight on the Thames across the road, with a daily walk in term-time of two miles or so in each direction, to the boys whose classical education at his hands enabled him to indulged his old passion for Homer, Theocritus, and Virgil, and whose games he urged on with the fervour of one who believed in the "Mens Sana in Corpore Sano" which hundreds of vanished preparatory schools have adopted as their guiding light.

Blackmore's life had followed this tranquil course for four years when he came into a substantial legacy from a maternal uncle which diverted it into the narrow road along which he was to journey for the remainder of his days. In 1857 he paid his Law Society dues, which had been outstanding for five years, and purchased a tract of land about eleven acres in extent, within a mile or so of Gomer House. The fact about the payment of the dues at this time is worthy of mention because it is inconceivable that Blackmore, who was a man of the most scrupulous honesty and conscientiousness, would not have settled this small sum earlier if he had had the means to do so. But now all was changed. He had money and a goodly parcel of English earth which he planned to make into a private Paradise, with a house of modest size containing one special sunlit room in which he would write to his heart's content, looking out on orchards and vineries that would bring to his imagination the opulent warmth of the cradle of civilized life.

The new "Gomer House" was ready for occupation in 1860. It was a square, double-fronted dwelling, plain and yet attractive in its utilitarian simplicity, not dissimilar in style to the "Max Gate" built by Thomas Hardy at Dorchester, Hardy having declared that he "was resolved not to ruin himself in building a great house as so many other literary men have done." A small room upstairs on the south side, subsequently to be half-covered by a magnificent magnolia-tree, he made his study. In the gardens he planted fruit-trees of superior quality, apples, pears, and apricots, peaches along the walls, and strawberries, currants and roses, in a profusion that made the place a memorable picture at blossom-time. That his crops never repaid, as a commercial venture, the immense labour and knowledge he bestowed upon them, was a bitter disappointment to him; but he had other rewards. There was the delighted eye of his visitors and the fact that he could hold his own with the experts in a discussion on the technicalities of fruit culture, the exciting possibilities of experiment and always the perverse but sincere pleasure of regarding himself more highly as a market-gardener than as a distinguished man of letters.

His early ventures in verse were followed in 1862 by a translation of the First and Second Georgics of Virgil, which Blackmore called *The Farm and Fruit of Old*. He took the manuscript personally to the publishers, Messrs. Sampson, Low, Son and Co., in Ludgate Hill, and Mr.

Edward Marston, who subsequently became a partner in the firm and an ever-encouraging friend, always remembered the voice of his caller as "gentle, deliberate, almost timid and yet manly." Blackmore's appearance at this time was probably very similar to that presented by him several years later to the few who were admitted to his private world—the square, rather stocky figure, with strong legs, a straight back, a fringe of beard of a traditionally bucolic nature round his chin, the shaggy eyebrows, and the clear gaze. The face that looks at us from a photograph taken in his middle-age is the face of a dreamer who yet has his feet on solid earth, a sagacious humanist of strong will and sometimes prejudiced determination. It is certain that Blackmore, who loved Virgil's themes, had a deep admiration for Virgil himself; the great poet's conviction of a Divine power at work in human affairs, his gentleness and reserved nature, and his moral ideals of self-mastery and fortitude, were shared by the novelist who gloried in the achievements of an Empire that surpassed even Virgil's Empire in wealth and power. Blackmore was pleased with his translation, but his habitual modesty did not allow him to say more than that "it was full of good work and lucky turns." He paid for this venture himself, and it was published anonymously. Those who bought it were probably surprised to read on the title-page that this translation in verse was by "A Market-Gardener". These slim volumes had appeared shyly in a world that was barely conscious of their presence, but they were not, in fact, the first considerable products of Blackmore's brain.

A year before the publication of *Poems by Melanter,* he had completed the manuscript of a novel and had put it aside.

A young man with Blackmore's imagination and feeling for words, who had a secret ambition to write the sort of novels which so many of his countrymen were producing with enormous success in the mid-century, could have been almost dazzled by the variety and range of the styles and topics offered to him as models, and by the number of his potential readers if he managed to achieve publication. There was a vast public hungry for fiction, in the form of the "three-decker" novel as supplied to the circulating libraries, as a serial in one of the numerous popular magazines, as a one-volume reprint, or as a cheap issue produced especially for the entertainment of travellers on the railways that were spreading now over the whole country. And the novel itself was undergoing immense expansion as a result of new materials and interests created by exploration and development in a hundred spheres. Dickens and Harrison Ainsworth, Charles Kingsley and Charlotte Brontë, Thackeray and Lord Lytton, as outstanding masters of a particular genre, represented a remarkably wide field of choice for a reader or a hopeful imitator with a pen.

There had also been growing up in France and America during the third and fourth decades of the century the novel of mystery and detection made according to the formula which has retained through a hundred years its primitive fascination. Vidocq's

Memoires, appearing in 1829, and crowded with accounts of his exploits as an agent of the Surêté, influenced a number of writers in his own country and in England, including Conan Doyle at a later period. In 1841 Edgar Allan Poe had produced *The Murders in the Rue Morgue.* By the time that Blackmore's *Clara Vaughan* was published, Wilkie Collins had written *The Dead Secret* and *The Woman in White,* and Le Fanu his *Ghost Stories of Chapelizod* and *The House by the Churchyard;* the Victorians now had a large, but never adequate, supply of a form of fiction that G. K. Chesterton called "a combination of the mechanical and mystical." And with the haunted twilights and the footprints in the earth came the bloodthirsty intruders from far-off Eastern countries; the "thug" was in fashion. He derived from a Hindu confraternity of professional assassins and robbers, specialists in strangling, who infested the central and northern parts of India during the early years of the century. They were eventually suppressed through strong measures taken by the British government between 1830 and 1835, but their fanaticism and sinister practices made them grand subjects for a novelist in search of a villain, and they were almost as common figures in Victorian fiction at one period as agents from Ruritania and Communist spies have been in later times.

We know that *Clara Vaughan* was in manuscript in 1853, because Blackmore himself has told us so in his preface to the revised edition of 1872. A good deal of it may therefore have been written as an antidote to the

Longworth Rectory, Berkshire, R. D. Blackmore's birthplace

tedium of his life as a student of the Middle Temple.
A review of the novel in "The Saturday Review" (April
30, 1864), after praising the book as "being occasionally
brilliant in flashes of fancy," had gone on to declare that
"the primary conception of the personages, the situations
in which they are introduced, and the tone of speech
and the sentiment throughout, are unmistakeably the
creation of a female mind." Blackmore assumed, as most
readers of the notice must also have assumed, that the
reviewer ascribed the authorship to Mrs. Braddon, whose
Lady Audley's Secret had leaped into phenomenal success two years before; if not by Mrs. Braddon herself,
the review implied that the novel had certainly been
written by a female slave of that "Queen of the Circulating Libraries". "Another decided feature", the reviewer continued, "by which our lady novelists are wont
to betray the secret of their authorship, is the characteristic mode in which they unconsciously make sport of the
simplest principles of physics, and of the most elementary
rules or usages of the law." This last criticism was surely
one which called forth the author's special indignation!
"I may be forgiven," says Blackmore, "for replying that
the story was in manuscript twenty years ago, save one;
and long before that lady's work created such a 'sen-
sation' in our recent world of literature."

Clara Vaughan, set chiefly in Gloucestershire, but
giving us glimpses of London and the North Devon area
Blackmore was to make so much his own, is told in the
first person singular by the determined and highly
emotional young lady who gives her name to the book.

The dominating passion of her life, stimulated by many a morbid reverie, is to discover the person who murdered her father in his bed shortly after the celebration of Clara's tenth birthday. By repeated visits to the scene of the crime Clara finds some clues which lead her into a number of sensational adventures, involving the disclosure of a Corsican vendetta, imprisonment in a vivisection chamber, and the sight of the violent end of the villain before wedding bells ring over her in the last chapter. The plot has no particular claim to originality, and there is a long story within the story which takes the reader off to Italy, and which for lushness and melodramatic sentimentality could not have been excelled by any contemporary authoress. But if the book has no memorable characters, it has its memorable moments. There is a magnificent description of the Western countryside in the long drought of 1849, and there are sketches of an "old-fashioned" Christmas and a London fog which could have come straight out of Dickens. The account of a wrestling-match between the Northern Champion and John Huxtable of Devon is a fine piece of writing, reminding us of the exceptional ability always shown by Blackmore in communicating the excitement of physical combat and the poetry of motion, whether of animal or man. But perhaps the special interest of the book is in its presentation of a character whose appearance in these pages makes Blackmore in a particular respect one of the pioneers.

The "detective" had now entered the English literary scene. In France Eugène Vidocq, the ex-convict who became a secret agent and later Chef de la Sûrêté, by publishing his *Memoires* (1828) had made himself into the first detective-hero the world has known. Not long afterwards Edgar Allan Poe, who read and appreciated Vidocq, created in M. Auguste Dupin the first detective to figure as the central character or "hero" of a work of fiction. In England the Bow Street Runners, of mixed reputattion, were superseded by the Metropolitan Police force, formed in 1829; fifteen years later the Home Secretary (Sir James Graham) decided to organise a team of a dozen "plain clothes detectives" to undertake criminal investigation as their special concern.

Charles Dickens, becoming very interested in this venture, interviewed a number of its leading officers and wrote several essays in 1850, and later, for "Household Words" about their activities and methods. He was highly enthusiastic about the scheme. "The Detective Force organised since the establishment of the existing Police, is so well chosen and trained, proceeds so systematically and quietly, does its business in such a workmanlike manner, and is always so calmly and steadily engaged in the service of the public, that the public really do not know enough of it, to know a tithe of its usefulness."

The public knew a good deal more very shortly, however, for Dickens wrote *Bleak House* as a serial which ran in "Household Words" in 1852 and 1853, and in Inspector Bucket he created the first police detective-hero in English fiction. "Dickens was the first novelist to portray the English police, their special place in the community they served, their organisations and the methods employed by the new 'detective force' symbolised by Inspector Bucket."[1] Four years before Wilkie Collins published *The Moonstone* (1868) with Sergeant Cuff, based on Inspector Whicher of Scotland Yard, as the man who plays the decisive part in the solution of the mystery, Blackmore, in *Clara Vaughan,* had produced his Inspector Cutting. As the first draft of the book was completed about twelve years earlier than its date of publication, Cutting must have been born in Blackmore's head at about the same time as Bucket in Dickens's. In view of the interest of this fact that Blackmore was one of the earliest English novelists to make use of the newly-created "Detective Force," our introduction to him ought to be quoted, together with his catechism of Clara in the manner with which hundreds of succeeding writers of "mysteries" have made us familiar :

> "Late in the evening she came to say that Inspector Cutting was there, and would come up if I wished it. Upon my request he came, and one look was enough to show that his niece had not misdescribed him. An elderly man, but active looking and wiry, with nothing remarkable in his features, except the clear cast of his forehead and the firm set of his mouth. But the quick intelligence that shot from his eyes made it seem waste of time to finish telling him anything. For this reason, polite though he was, it became unpleasant to talk to him. It was something like shooting at divers—as my father used

[1] *The Development of the Detective Novel,* by A. E. Murch.

to describe it—for whom the flash of the gun is enough.

Yet he never once stopped or hurried me, until my tale was done, and all my thoughts laid bare. Then he asked me to see all my relics and vestiges of the dead; even my gordit did not escape him.

'L.D.O.' he said shortly, 'do you speak Italian?'

'I can read it, but not speak it.'

'Is it commoner for Italian surnames to begin with an O, or with a C?'

'There are plenty beginning with both; but more I should think with a C.'

When all my particulars had been told, and all my evidence shown, I asked with breathless interest—for my confidence in him grew fast—what his opinion was.

'Allow me, young lady, to put a few questions to you, on matters you have not mentioned. Forgive me, if they pain you. I believe you feel that they will not be impertinent.'

I promised to answer without reserve.

'What was your mother's personal appearance?'

'Most winning and delicate.'

'How old was she at the time of her marriage?'

'Twenty-one, I believe.'

'How old was your father then?'

'Twenty-five.'

'How many years were they married?'

'Sixteen exactly.'

'When did your guardian first leave England?'

'In the course of a year or two after the marriage.'

'Had there been any misunderstanding between him and your father?'

'None, that I ever heard of.'

37

'Did your father, at any time, travel on the continent?'

'Only in Switzerland, and part of Italy, during his wedding tour.'

'Your guardian returned, I believed, at intervals to England?' I had never told him this.

'Yes. At least I suppose so, or he would not have been in London.'

'Did he visit them at Vaughan Park?'

'Not once, within my memory.'

'Thank you. I will ask no more. It is a strange story; but I have known several much more strange. Of one thing be assured. I shall catch the criminal.' "

When one adds that later on Inspector Cutting opens a locked door with a skeleton key, searches for the minutest clues, and disguises himself so thoroughly that even Clara finds it difficult to recognise him, it will be seen that he comes very close to the pattern of the traditional "sleuth" as we have come to know him.

The book has one other distinction and point of interest. Blackmore succeeded, in his creation of Clara Vaughan, in making a heroine who is more real and living to us than any other of the many heroines he produced from a single mould of celestial perfection. Many years later he told a friend that he "knew two people who prefer Clara to the more popular Lorna." Their reason must have been that Clara Vaughan, long since lost in the oblivion of minor Victorian literature, reveals at least one or two of the faults common to our imperfect human nature; whereas the immortal Lorna Doone apparently has none to show.

III

IF Clara Vaughan had been a great success, Blackmore would have been as delighted as any other writer of a first novel that has pleased reviewers and readers alike, but he did not allow its very lukewarm reception to affect in any way the course he had planned for his life at Teddington.

He spent the mornings in his garden, planting, pruning, appraising the progress of new types of fruit-trees, and making notes about his experiments for the benefit of botanically-inclined friends and horticultural journals. Beside his house he built a pigeon-loft, and occasionally in the evenings he went down to the village headquarters of the Thames Valley Chess Club. He was a great walker, and close at hand were Bushey Park and Richmond Park and the river towpath, to give him all the exercise he needed. But his special happiness was always here behind the stout walls of his little kingdom; the inspiration of his love and his sunny room, the first blossoms, the thought, lighting his mind and his inner life with the intensity of religious faith, of that eternal golden age in which the lover and his lass stand for ever in the meadows of their first meeting. Outside those walls was a world which did not interest him greatly, and he did not expect it or want to be interested in him. The world was, as a matter of fact, chiefly interested at this moment in the rumpus over the Reform Bills and the trial of Constance Kent for the alleged murder of a child in a lonely house in Wiltshire.

For the setting of his next novel Blackmore came nearer to his adopted home in choosing the New Forest area around Lyndhurst and Ringwood, and again he chose for his title (*Cradock Nowell*) the name of one of the chief characters in the story. Nearly all his later novels bore on their title-page the name of their hero or heroine—*Lorna Doone, Alice Lorraine, Cripps the Carrier, Mary Anerley, and Dariel*. In one case both were combined in *Kit and Kitty*. Charles Dickens followed the same course with *Nicholas Nickleby, Oliver Twist, Martin Chuzzlewit, Edwin Drood, Barnaby Rudge,* and *Dombey and Son*. One recalls, too, *Henry Esmond, Richard Feverel, Evan Harrington, Henrietta Temple, Adam Bede, Jane Eyre* and *Mary Barton*. There is surely a deep significance in this fact. For the Victorians the human being was the centre and goal of the work of creation; and although the more fortunate of them did not customarily act as if they regarded all other human beings as important as themselves, theoretically they believed the world to be revolving round the individual, and his or her choice of action, for good or evil, as the eternally dramatic event in which God took an even stronger interest than the novelist or the preacher. The ages of faith are always ages in which the person counts, and the fact is advertised for all time in the Church's calendar of saints. There were clouds on the Victorian religious horizon, produced by the challenge of Darwin and the growth of a liberal party in the

Church itself, but the great majority of her people lived their lives against a background of God's holy will and purpose which they may often have defied or ignored, but never seriously questioned. Things had not moved far in those days towards the making of those "acids of modernity" which have eaten into the ancient vessels of the Faith. Turn to the titles of three score of the novels that have made their mark in recent years, and one will scarcely find any that do not reflect our changed emphasis. "Things are in the saddle and ride mankind."

The years between the writing of *Clara Vaughan* and the publication of *Cradock Nowell* were marked by the appearance of a great number of popular magazines as rivals of the periodicals of high literary and intellectual merit. "Macmillan's Magazine" was born in 1859—a year so remarkable in the importance and variety of the outstanding works it produced, that it must be unique in this regard in our literary history. In 1859 appeared Darwin's *Origin of Species,* George Eliot's *Adam Bede,* Tennyson's *Idylls of the King,* Smiles's *Self Help,* Dickens's *A Tale of Two Cities,* and Meredith's *The Ordeal of Richard Feverel.* Immediately after "Macmillan's" came "The Cornhill", and then a great number of magazines like "Temple Bar", "Belgravia", and "Tinsley's Magazine," all of which aimed chiefly at a public that wanted reading of the lighter sort. This type of magazine dealt the death-blow to the "part-issue" form of publication which had been popular for nearly forty years, and then itself eventually succumbed to the new hordes of illustrated monthlies (like "The Strand") which came out in the last decade of the century. The fiction in serial form carried by the majority of these magazines provided an opportunity of publication denied to aspiring authors in our own day, which has seen the decease of all such ventures, with the notable exception of "Cornhill" and "Blackwood". *Cradock Nowell* was accepted for serialisation in "Macmillan's Magazine" between May, 1865, and August, 1866. Malcolm Irwin, in his book *Victorian Wallflowers,* is probably right in maintaining that the cold reception accorded to all of Blackmore's novels except *Lorna Doone,* and the oblivion into which they have since fallen, is due to his writing in the wake of a departing vogue. Blackmore could not and would not supply the kind of sensationalism and romantic absurdity wanted by the great multitude of readers of Mrs. Henry Wood, Ouida, and Miss Braddon.

The plot of *Cradock Nowell* is unoriginal and clumsy, and in essence may be found in many other novels of the period. The story is hinged upon the fact that the twin sons of the owner of the great estate of Nowelhurst were confused by a nurse shortly after their birth. Cradock had expected to be the heir before the error was discovered, and when his brother Clayton is shot close to a place where Cradock is hunting, suspicion inevitably falls upon the latter. The problem of the disputed inheritance is one that Blackmore used in his plots several times, and the fact is not really surprising. There had been litigation in his own family, and he had had plenty of examples in his legal training to provide him with good material in this line. Judging from the extent to which lawyers and their disputing clients figure in the great mass of Victorian fiction, few citizens of that period had no experience of the courts and their preliminaries.

Blackmore had no initial success to follow up when he wrote *Cradock Nowell,* and his second effort made no better impression than his first. The critics were severe, and in a one-volume edition published in 1873 Blackmore appended to the title the words, in parenthesis: "Diligently Revised and Reshapen". With his customary humility he announced in the preface to this edition that the reviewers had found him guilty of "obscurity, want of proportion, crudeness, imperfect development, pedantry, involution of diction, and prolixity". He adds sadly that a new book might have been written while the old one was a-mending; "but half the value of discipline consists in mortification".

A modern reader who persevered through even a quarter of the revised novel's sixty-four chapters might wonder what the original version could have been like, if this was less prolix and Blackmore here less guilty of "involution of diction"! The long sentences, the many digressions, the scores of classical allusions and quotations, must render the book unreadable today by any except those who can endure such things for the sake of the occasional felicities of description of field and forest, in which Blackmore was so comfortably at home. He can never in *Cradock Nowell,* and but rarely in his other novels, speak simply of a simple person, but must expend to the full every image and every comparison in relation to that person which comes into his mind; he is so determined to make us picture the unearthly charm of his heroine or the manly power of his hero that he takes us and stuns us with such a force of adjectives and similes that we are left in no condition to perceive a creature of flesh and blood at all.

Similar criticisms about digression and an involuted style were being made at this time about the work of George Meredith. Meredith did of course indulge in much artificial diction, but his verboseness is constantly redeemed by the sound psychological insight and unsentimental delineation of character which we find as the reward of going on. Both Meredith and Blackmore were lovers of life, enraptured by the fecundity and delicacy of Spring, and both fundamentally optimists, the one sustained by a pantheistic earth-mysticism and the other by the doctrines of the Protestant Church. But notice the difference between Meredith and Blackmore when they place their heroine in an appropriate setting and surround her with the natural beauty they understood so well. Here is our introduction to Amy Rosedew in *Cradock Nowell* :

"Early on a sunripe evening in the month of June, when the sun was shifting the shadows of the hills, and doffed the jaded oxen's yoke, distributing the lovetime from his waning chariot', a forest dell, soft, clear, and calm, was listening to its thrushes. And more than at the throstle's flute, or flagelot of the blackbird, oaks and chestnuts pricked their ears at the voice of a gliding maiden. Where the young tern

44

was pluming itself, arching, lifting, ruffling in fiili-
gree, light perspective, and depth of Gothic tracery,
freaked by the nip of fairy fingers, tremulous as a
coral grove in a crystal under-current, the shyer
fronds still nestling home, uncertain of the world as
yet, and coiled like catherine-wheels of green; where
the cranesbill pushed like Zedekiah, and the succory
reared its sky-blue windmill (open for business till
8 p.m.); where the violet now was rolled up in the
seed-pod, like a stylite millipede, and the great bind-
weed, in its crenate horn, piped and fluted spirally,
had forgotten its noonday flaunt; here, and over the
nibbled sward, where the crisp dew was not risen
yet, here came wandering the lightest foot that ever
passed, but shook not, the moss-bed of the glow-
worm. Under the rigorous oaks (so corded, seamed,
and wenned with humps of grey), the stately sleek,
mouse-coloured beech, the dappled moss-beridden
ash, and the birch-tree peeling silverly, beneath the
murmuring congress of the sunproof leaves ; and
again in the open breaks and valleys, where light and
shade went see-saw; by and through and under all,
feeling for and with every one, glanced, and gleamed,
and glistened and listened the loveliest being where
all was love, the pet in the nest of nature.

Of all the beauty in that sweet dell, where the
foot of man came scarcely once in a year; of all the
largesse of earth and heaven; of all the grace which
is Nature's gratitude to her heavenly Father; there
was not one, from the lily-bell to the wild rose and
the heather-sprig, fit for a man to put in his bosom,
and look at Amy Rosedew."

The reader is certainly not permitted to look at her,
for the rest of the chapter is in exactly similar strain, and

45

she does not emerge as anything more definite than a "shy and graceful maiden" who might be any one of Blackmore's other numerous heroines. Compare this with our introduction to Lucy in *The Ordeal of Richard Feverel*:

"Above green-flashing plunges of a weir, and shaken by the thunder below, lilies, golden and white, were swaying at anchor among the reeds. Meadowsweet hung from the banks thick with weed and trailing bramble, and there also hung a daughter of earth. Her face was shaded by a broad straw hat with a flexible brim that left her lips and chin in the sun, and, sometimes nodding, sent forth a light of promising eyes. Across her shoulders, and behind, flowed large loose curls, brown in shadow, almost golden where the ray touched them. She was simply dressed, befitting decency and the season . . . The little skylark went up above her, all song, to the smooth southern cloud lying along the blue : from a dewy copse dark over her nodding hat the blackbird fluted, calling to her with thrice mellow note : the kingfisher flashed emerald out of green osiers; a bow-winged heron travelling aloft, seeking solitude : a boat slipped toward her, containing a dreamy youth; and still she plucked her fruit, and ate, and mused, as if no fairy prince were invading her territories, and as if she wished not for one, or knew not her wishes. Surrounded by the green shaven meadows, the pastoral summer buzz, the weirfall's thundering white, amid the breath and beauty of wild flowers, she was a bit of lovely human life in a fair setting; a terrible attraction."

R. D. BLACKMORE AND HIS NOVELS

Such splendid sensuousness, driven powerfully home in the last three words, was beyond Blackmore's accomplishment. If he believed privately that sexual passion can be sacramental, as Meredith undoubtedly believed, he was so busy showing his readers the inward and spiritual graces that they could gain little idea of it ; for the outward and visible signs are largely ignored. It is in a sense symbolic of Blackmore's attitude as a writer that when Cradock Nowell espies Amy coquetting with her image in the forest pool he immediately remembers that he is a gentleman—and goes away.

Cradock Nowell has some magnificent passages, especially in the long description of a storm in the New Forest. Conrad never drew a storm at sea more vividly than Blackmore has painted this one in a series of pictures, beginning with the "blobs of cloud" which "threw feelers out, and strung themselves together, until a broad serried and serrate bar went boldly across the heavens." At the end the reader is left breathless from the fury of a storm that has smashed and wrecked and killed from Christchurch to the Goodwins. Blackmore was as apt at describing the violence of nature as the violence of man, and the digressions which ruin so many of his novels find no place when he has his eyes on bending trees or straining limbs.

In the Rev. John Rosedew, Rector of the little New Forest parish of Nowellhurst, Blackmore has created a country parson of the finest type. He is the servant of the simple, the bosom-friend of the Squire, the beloved friend and pastor of his small self-contained community,

47

with a good taste in wines, an accomplished classic, a man who can swim and fish and row and (with some misgivings proceeding from his Christian charity) also shoot. "In all the parish of Nowellhurst there was scarcely a man or a woman who did not rejoice to see the rector pacing his leisurely rounds, carrying his elbows a little out, as men with large deltoid muscles do, wearing his old hat far back on his head, so that it seemed to slope away from him, and smiling gently upon the children who tugged his coat-tails for an orange or a halfpenny." He is the figure in the rural scene whom Thomas Hardy has completely forgotten. There were too many parsons of another sort (and Blackmore had met them), but the John Rosedews have existed and their influence has been a large factor in shaping a way of life that had the roots our civilisation so tragically lacks. In *Cradock Nowell* Blackmore affirms the robust Christianity, the personal and enthusiastic conviction of an essential justice and purpose in the world, which Browning was proclaiming in his poetry. As one reads about Rosedew, one is reminded of the words of Professor Herbert Butterfield in his analysis of history and the Church:[1] "If people would turn . . . from politico-ecclesiastical history to the intimate life of the Church throughout the ages, and the spiritual work done by humble men over the face of the continent for fifteen hundred years, they would find it the most moving spectacle that history presents, and would see how the spread of piety does mean a growth in charity."

[1] *Christianity and History.*

Unfortunately, however, for the nineteenth-century reader, and fatally for the reader of to-day, Parson Rosedew, "who always thought in Greek, except when Latin hindered him", is made the mouthpiece of Blackmore's own classical erudition. The Greek and Latin references and quotations run into scores, and Blackmore, until he had learned a little more about readers who had neither a University education nor a personal library, scorned to translate.

So *Cradock Nowell* made only a very slight ripple in the wide sea of Victorian fiction, and Blackmore went on with his pruning and his planting and his chess-playing. It was enough for him that his "dear friend, Thomas James Scalé" had taken the kindest interest in the story from month to month, and some portion of a large debt of gratitude to his old Headmaster had thereby been discharged. And already his imagination was busy with the outlines of another story. Blackmore went off for a holiday to North Devon, to get certain features of the homeland of his ancestors more clearly imprinted on his mind.

D

IV

BLACKMORE's Devon days were far away and long ago, but he did not forget them. The topographical variety of his novels seems to show that any corner of wild and lonely English countryside evoked his affections as strongly as the region of the west he has made his own. Nine of Blackmore's novels are set in nine different counties, and although with *Perlycross,* written six years before his death, he came back to Somerset, the success of *Lorna Doone* did not induce him to become a "regional" novelist. A holiday in Devon, however, brought strongly back to him some of his dearest memories, and in a fugitive magazine called "The Leisure Hour" he found a story entitled "The Doones of Exmoor". The account of the band of robbers who had made a stronghold at Badgworthy and had terrorised all in the surrounding countryside had been among the "nurse tales" of his childhood; and in something of that old fear and fascination the finest of his works was forged. It is not difficult to imagine the excitement, coupled with many diversionary musings as he recalled his early days in the wonderland now two hundred miles away from him, which possessed Blackmore as he wrote down in exercise books in his neat but tiny hand, the adventures of John Ridd and Lorna Doone, feeling that now the die was cast for him as a novelist, and that (as he told his publisher afterwards) if this book, into which he was putting his best work, should fail, little

51

heart would be left in him for trying any other.

It is perhaps worthy of mention today that the only edition of *Lorna Doone* that will enable a reader to experience its full flavour and to find the deepest pleasure in the character-drawing, the descriptive passages, and the record of vanished customs, is an edition of the book as Blackmore wrote it. The fashion of "abridgement" and "outline" (not to speak of the "strip-cartoon") which is considered necessary for twentieth-century men reared on headlines, and which has laid its dead hand on this as on scores of other victims in the ranks of major literature, has meant that a great number of modern readers have never read, and never will read, the novel that is called *Lorna Doone*. Wireless and the cinema can satisfy the customers who know the title, and are willing to give an hour or so to knowing a little more, by making it a melodrama about gangsters or an appendage to a "realistically-produced" Battle of Sedgemoor. Even the prefix to the story (a quotation from the eighth Idyll of Theocritus) has disappeared from modern editions, original or translation both being denied to the reader who might be glad to realise at the outset that the book celebrates the eternal and satisfying simplicities which were so dear to Blackmore himself :

"No wide domain, nor golden treasure,
  Nor speed like wind across the lea,
I pray for : here I find my pleasure,
  In this cliff shade embracing thee,
My grazing sheep to watch at leisure,
  And sing to yon Sicilian sea."

52

LORNA DOONE:

A Romance of Exmoor.

By R. D. BLACKMORE,

AUTHOR OF 'CRADOCK NOWELL,' ETC.

Μή μοι γᾶν Πέλοπος, μή μοι χρύσεια τάλαντα
Εἴη ἔχεν, μηδὲ πρόσθε θέειν ἀνέμων·
Ἀλλ' ὑπὸ τᾷ πέτρᾳ τᾷδ' ἀσομαι, ἀγκὰς ἔχων τυ,
Σύννομα μᾶλ' ἐσορῶν τὰν Σικελὰν ἐς ἅλα.

IN THREE VOLUMES.

VOL. I.

LONDON:

SAMPSON LOW, SON, & MARSTON,

CROWN BUILDINGS, 188, FLEET STREET.

1869.

Title-page of the first edition of *Lorna Doone*, a copy of
which was sold for £200 in 1936.

(*By kind permission of Maggs Bros.*)

But the publishers' readers were not impressed. When
finally Sampson, Low accepted the manuscript, the firm
appears to have done so largely because of the friendship between Mr. Low and the author, rather than from
any confidence in its success, as only five hundred copies
were printed, in three volumes. When the publisher
risked a one-volume edition in 1872, a misinformed
journalist declared that the book concerned the family
of "the bridegroom of the hour"—the Marquis of Lorne,
whose marriage with Princess Louise (daughter of Queen
Victoria) aroused a great deal of public interest. The
public accepted this as a fact, and a demand for copies
was awakened at once. Blackmore, who must have
known as surely as anyone else with some sense in his
head that a great book's intrinsic merits are bound to
be recognised sooner or later, himself maintained that
this was the real reason for suddenly finding himself a
"best-selling" novelist; and to some extent the for-
tuitous manner of the book's sudden popularity added to
his irritation in later years at the way in which his other
novels languished in the shade of his masterpiece. Hence-
forth in the public mind Blackmore was simply the
author of *Lorna Doone* as Daniel Defoe was the man
who wrote only *Robinson Crusoe*.

In his *Aspects of the Novel,* E. M. Forster says that
"the final test of a novel will be our affection for it,
as it is the test of our friends, and of anything else which
we cannot define." But while love may be blind on the
part of the common reader, the critic, sharing his affection, can discover and discuss the various features which

have produced the endearing quality, and in *Lorna Doone* they are evident at once. With his theme and his chief characters Blackmore struck the chord that mankind is always longing to hear; in this book surely is the quintessence of the "nurse tales" of the world's own childhood. And dominating all is the universal appeal of the hero and heroine; for the contrast between the unlearned but good-hearted giant and the ethereal charm of the young girl pleasantly ratifies our deep-seated ideals about sexual characteristics. "That is the way things are, and if not, they ought to be."

When the book was reviewed in "The Athenaeum" of April 17, 1869, the reviewer had declared that "the story is well-told . . . and narrated in a quiet and veracious style, with unconscious touches of character and the introduction of persons who are not only historical but life-like." The last presumably refers to Judge Jeffreys and King James, and is not taken as implying that the writer included the Doones and Tom Faggus in the "historical" category. But it was just this matter of "life-likeness" which troubled the author of a lengthy review of the book in the "Saturday Review" of November 5, 1870. Having saluted *Lorna Doone* as a work "of real excellence, though we do not pretend to rank it with the acknowledged masterpieces of fiction," he went on to his chief point of criticism:

"The character of Lorna is very beautiful, if more ideal, and therefore impossible; and her constancy to her faithful, slow-going yeoman, who divides his time between her and his beasts, and dwells on his

passion while plodding between his furrows, is very
tenderly worked out . . . Yet, charming as she is, if
we were inclined to take grave exception to anything
in the book, it would be to this very character of Lorna; not because it is not beautiful, but
because it is not natural. She is as purely imaginary,
as purely unreal from the point of view of humanity,
as one of Moore's angels or Arab girls. She is one
of those creatures, much delighted in by romancists,
who are independent of education, and owe nothing
to training; one of those self-perfecting, self-sufficing
women who grow up pure, refined, and accomplished
in the midst of vice, vulgarity, and neglect; and on
whom outside conditions have no kind of effect, and
spiritual tendencies are the sole modifying forces."

This, of course, is true. When John Ridd first met
Lorna coming to him among the primroses he "could
not see what her face was", and neither can we, then
or ever afterwards. But here Blackmore's usual failure to
convey the form and features of his heroine is surely one
of the reasons for the story's perennial appeal. For what
we do with Lorna is to draw her as we wish. She may
indeed be the fictional counterpart of one of Kate Green-
away's innocent maidens in white muslin and a pink
sash, as ethereal in her frail femininity as Charles Lamb's
Rosamund Grey. It is enough for us that "Young Allan
Clare, when but a boy, sighed for her." She is every
man's goddess, whose face and peculiar tenderness he can
create for himself. That woman is of the earth, earthy,
modern novelists have left us in no doubt whatever; we
ought to know by now that the heroine will have firm

breasts and damp armpits, and that pedestals were marks of a particularly Victorian vulgarity. Yet in the heart of every man is the persisting dream, the stubborn refusal to acknowledge (however often he may be told to keep his feet and his eyes firmly on the ground) that the Fall has left as deep a mark upon *her* as upon *him*:

> She is what my heart, awaking,
> Whisper'd the world was. Morning light is she.

And, turning from the sublime to the infernal, what more possibly fascinating and haunting villains than the Doones are there in all literature? Blackmore believed that they had a local habitation and a name, and roundly declared, to the scorn of those who were not there to see and so must reserve their judgement, that certain grim incidents connected with them were true "beyond a doubt". The question is an academic one, and is unlikely ever to be satisfactorily answered. If the Doones did not exist, an acquaintance with those shadowed combes and windy paths going off into mystery will create them there—in the proper place for villains who chime with our earliest memories of what proper villains should be. Is not Carver Doone as unforgettable as Quilp and Fagin?

Fortunately displayed, too, in *Lorna Doone* is Blackmore's habit of mixing fact and fancy concerning persons and places. He declared long afterwards that if he could have foreseen the great success of the book, he would have taken pains to indicate more clearly the location

of certain scenery and buildings mentioned in it, but it
is difficult to see why he need have felt such compulsion.
The identification of an "exact spot" (especially if it is
associated with tragedy) may lengthen the queue of sight-
seers, but it does little to increase the reader's delight
in a romance like *Lorna Doone,* whose author made no
claim to accuracy of this kind. Blackmore's method in
Lorna Doone balances the interesting delineation of the
"recognised" with the attractive "mystery" of that which
we cannot positively discover. It is much better that
people should still be seeking for the original of Plover's
Barrows Farm than that they should have turned it
long since into a tea-house and a postcard-counter.[1]

There is scarcely a chapter in the long book which
does not offer something worthy of quotation as a piece
of magnificent descriptive writing, but some passages
stand out particularly as examples of Blackmore's power
in communicating to us situations of drama and suspense,
especially in the ardours and excitements of physical
action. Take, for instance, the glorious vigour and crisp
realism of his account of John Ridd's battle with Tom
Faggus's strawberry mare :

"First she reared upright in the air, and struck
me full on the nose with her comb, till I bled worse
than Robin Snell made me; and then down with her
fore-feet deep in the straw, and her hind-feet going
to heaven. Finding me stick to her still like wax (for

[1] "Lorna Doone Farm" at Malmstead is not John Ridd's home-
stead. The latter may have been at the present Oare Ford
Farm.

58

my mettle was up as hers was) away she flew with
me, swifter than ever I went before, or since, I trow.
She drove full-head at the cobwall—'Oh, Jack, slip
off,' screamed Annie—then she turned like light,
when I thought to crush her, and ground my left
knee against it. 'Mux me,' I cried for my breeches
were broken, and short words went the furthest—'if
you kill me, you shall die with me.' Then she took the
court-yard gate at a leap, knocking my words between my teeth, and then right over a quickset
hedge, as if the sky were a breath to her; and away
for the water-meadows, while I lay on her neck like
a child at the breast, and wished I had never been
born. Straight away, all in the front of the wind, and
scattering clouds around her, all I knew of the speed
we made was the frightful flash of her shoulders,
and her mane like trees in a tempest. I felt the earth
under us rushing away, and the air left far behind
us, and my breath came and went, and I prayed to
God, and was sorry to be so late of it.

All the long swift while, without power of thought,
I clung to her crest and shoulders, and dug my nails
into her creases, and my toes into her flank-part,
and was proud of holding on so long, though sure of
being beaten. Then in her fury at feeling me still,
she rushed at another device for it, and leaped the
wide water-trough sideways across, to and fro, till
no breath was left in me. The hazel-boughs took me
too hard in the face, and the tall dog-briars got hold
of me, and the ache of my back was like crimping
a fish; till I longed to give up, and lay thoroughly
beaten, and lie there and die in the cresses. But there
came a shrill whistle from up the home-hill, where
the people had hurried to watch us; and the mare
stopped as if with a bullet; then set off for home

with the speed of a swallow, and going as smoothly
and silently. I never had dreamed of such delicate
motion, fluent, and graceful, and ambient, soft as the
breeze flitting over the flowers, but swift as the
summer lightning. I sat up again, but my strength
was all spent, and no time left to recover it; and at
last, as she rose at our gate like a bird, I tumbled off
into the mixen."

And how perfectly, in contrasting mood, the lover's
anxieties are framed in the heedless changes and beauties
of nature as John Ridd sorrows over Lorna's long and
unexplained absence from their trysting-place :

"Perhaps it is needless for me to say, that all this
time, while my month was running—or rather
crawling, for never month went so slow as that with
me—neither weed, nor seed, nor cattle, nor my own
mother's anxiety, nor any care for my sister, kept
me from looking once every day, and even twice on
a Sunday, for any sign of Lorna. For my heart was
ever weary; in the budding valleys, and by the
crystal waters, looking at the lambs in fold, or the
heifers on the hill, labouring in trickled furrows, or
among the beaded blades; halting fresh to see the
sun light over the golden-vapoured ridge; or doffing
hat, from sweat of brow, to watch him sink in the
low grey sea; be it as it would, of day, of work, or
night, or slumber, it was a weary heart I bore, and
fear was on the brink of it.

All the beauty of the spring went for happy men
to think of; all the increase of the year was for other
eyes to mark. Not a sign of any sunrise for me, from
my fount of life; not a breath to stir the dead leaves
fallen on my heart's Spring."

R. D. BLACKMORE AND HIS NOVELS

In contrast to such felicities the book has its weaknesses, but they are not those of plot and prolixity which so often brought upon Blackmore the reviewer's stern judgment. The conferring of a knighthood on John Ridd must strike many readers as unconvincing and out of harmony with the spirit of the tale; justice and righteousness would have been equally well served, one feels, if we had taken leave of John without a title and Lorna without a fortune. The brief glimpse of the Battle of Sedgemoor, the details of which Blackmore had evidently taken from Macaulay, shows us little that is memorable, and the account of its aftermath slips sadly into bathos. The rugged structure of the prose, with its many passages of unforced lyricism, is sometimes broken into by rhythm which sounds oddly in the context. Here, for example, the reader might think himself suddenly to have wandered into Longfellow's "Hiawatha": "Much abashed with joy was I, when I saw my Lorna coming, purer than the morning dew, than the sun more bright and clear." Elsewhere one finds several metres mingled, and there is frequent use of alliteration; facts which Dr. Burris thinks may be due to Blackmore's regular reading of the Bible and of the Norse sagas which were popular at this time.

The truth remains that the book as a whole reaches a level which Blackmore was never quite able to attain in any of his other works; we are aware on every page that he lost himself more thoroughly in its composition and felt more passionately the sadness and sweetness of life in the story of John and Lorna than was the case with any of his other books. The greatest novels are probably always created in nostalgia. In *Lorna Doone* imagination is nourished by memory; and we find ourselves believing that somewhere in a remote past all this happened to *us;* the glens and lovely combes of Exmoor are an Eden from which in our soiled mid-life we have been banished, but to which one day we shall be allowed to return. Was it the sense that Blackmore had conducted them to a lost Paradise that led many writers, not known to be enamoured of romantic simplicities, to express their gratitude for *Lorna Doone*? Thirty years later even the egregious Frank Harris, whose character Blackmore must thoroughly have despised if he had known about it, sent a copy of *Elder Conklin,* inscribed "to the author of John Ridd, from one of his admirers."

V

Lorna Doone brought Blackmore some money that he greatly needed. For some time he had been losing heavily on his commercial fruit-growing. He marketed his fruit for forty years, and only twice did he succeed in making both ends meet. In one year he lost nearly £500. He had difficulty in getting adequate staff, and there was the constant bugbear of inclement weather. He made careful and most detailed daily notes about climatic conditions, kept a rainfall gauge, and left clear evidence that Victorian summers were not, as we are apt to suppose, generally kinder than our own. There were also losses incurred by the slackness and carelessness of his gardeners, from whom Blackmore demanded the unquestioning and diligent service which Victorian employers of labour were accustomed to expect from those whom God had called to their particular station in life. In one case he suffered heavily through an act of terrible vindictiveness. Some years after Blackmore's death an anonymous correspondent in a publishers' journal recalled the incident, about which he had heard on a visit to Gomer House :

> "Anger can be calm, and we never saw a better proof of this than when he showed us in his vineries glaring proof of as despicable an act of revenge as can well be imagined. He was essentially kind-hearted, but his patience and unavailing extension of forgiveness towards a gardener in his employ at

last came to an end, and the man had to go. Wondering why after their winter rest his beloved vines showed no signs of life, he opened up the earth round the stem of one and found it had been severed some depth below the surface, and this was the case with all, and so in one night, the loving care of years, and many of the finest grape-vines in the country—prize-winners—were destroyed."

Blackmore now began work on another novel, for which he had made some notes in his younger days. He had spent many of his school holidays at Nottage Court, in Glamorganshire, a Tudor manor house which had been the home of his mother's people for several generations; not far away from it, on the edge of the sandhills outside Porthcawl, is Sker House, a large Elizabethan mansion, perhaps originally a monastery, and now a farm. Porthcawl, once a coal-port of some importance, has become a flourishing seaside resort, and the Glamorganshire coast has yielded much of its old beauty to the necessities of industry and the habits of holiday-makers, but Blackmore knew and loved the unspoilt countryside of his day, with its fine stretches of lonely sand along the rugged coast, and the view across the Channel of the great bluffs of Exmoor.

The story, of which the incidents take place a hundred years after Lorna Doone, is told by a kind but somewhat cunning fisherman named Davy Llewellyn, who on one of his expeditions finds a two-year-old girl asleep in a boat which has apparently just drifted to shore. He keeps both the boat and the child, the former to help him in his fishing, and the latter as a companion for his grand-daughter. When the fish-harvest is poor, Davy leaves the children in charge of a schoolmaster, and gets a job on a trading-vessel. He soon, however, becomes an employee of one Parson Chowne. The parson, wielding a double power as clergyman and landowner, is a most fearsome creation; he keeps savage dogs, a horde of naked and slug-eating servants on his forty acres, horsewhips his enemies, and practises witchcraft. Davy soon found that he had been really hired to act as a spy on the inhabitants of Narnton Court, the estate of Sir Philip Bampfylde, who for some time had been searching for a lost grandson. There was local suspicion that both his child and a twin female child had been abducted by Parson Chowne, but the minister sought to fasten his crime upon Drake Bampfylde, younger son of Sir Philip and uncle of the twins. Drake's motive, it was suggested, was to get the baronetcy and the estates for himself. Drake went to sea, but came back at intervals to see Isabel Carey, his father's ward, upon whom the parson had designs of his own. Chowne sought to keep alive the suspicion against Drake, in the hope that the lovers would become estranged. Davy at last could stand the violence and insolence of Chowne no longer, and went over to Isabel's employ, acting sometimes as a spy on his former master. When open war broke out between the two men, Davy joined the Navy under Captain Drake, but often came back to see his charges and to visit Isabel for news. It was during such a period that the exposure of the abductor came about quite acciden-

65

E

tally. Some dogs unearthed a naval hat that had been stolen from Drake, and two dolls, and one of the people living in squalor on Chowne's land testified to having seen a man with a naval hat digging a grave on the beach in the dusk, but could not be sure of his identity. Some time later Davy came to the colony of savages in quest of recruits for his ship, and of the four men he took away one proved to be the son of Philip Bamfylde, abducted long ago with his sister at the instance of Parson Chowne. The girl had accidentally floated away in a boat, and proved of course to be none other than Bardie, whom Davy had discovered. Chowne thereupon retired to his farm, and met a terrible end through his own violence, for in a fit of enormous rage he struck one of his dogs, which turned and bit him, so that he died of rabies as a raving madman. Drake married Isabel, and Davy leaves the scene with a double pension and the gift of a fine craft, built at Appledore, which he calls "Maid of Sker".

It is difficult to understand why a number of critics, and indeed Blackmore himself, have held this novel in such high esteem. The plot strains the reader's credulity, and relies on chances and coincidences even more strongly than *Cradock Nowell*. The striking descent from *Lorna Doone* in this respect is evident also in the character-drawing. The child Bardie is Blackmore's contribution to the gallery of frail and frilly children produced in the romantic period. "The literary climate in which the Romantic child developed was prepared in the half-century from Rousseau's 'Emile' to Wordworth's

'Prelude'."[1] Bardie, appearing at almost the same time as Paul Dombey, comes trailing the clouds of glory which Blackmore, himself childless, believed in passionately :

> "Because she was so fast asleep, and that alone is something holy in a very little child; so much it seems to be the shadow of the death itself, in their pausing, fluttering lives, in their want of wit for dreaming, and their fitness for a world of which they must know more than this; also to a man who feels the loss of much believing, and what grievous gain it is to make doubt of everything, such a simple trust in Him, than whom we find no better father, such a confidence of safety at the very outset seems a happy art unknown, and tempts him back to ignorance. Well aware what years must bring, from all the ill they have brought to us, we cannot watch this simple sort without a sadness on our side, a pity, and a longing as for something lost and gone."

Bardie is the incarnation of holiness as Parson Chowne is the incarnation of evil, but the latter is too melodramatically overdrawn to terrify us, and it is certain that Bardie's "quaintness" will be judged by most modern readers to be tedious whimsy.

Sentiments and opinions are put into the mouth of old Davy which he could never have expressed as Blackmore, so obviously speaking in many instances through the sailor's lips, makes him express them. But it is interesting to have in this way further glimpses into Black-

[1] *Poor Monkey (The Child in Literature)*, by Peter Coveney.

more's mind, and into the spirit and outlook we call
Victorianism. There is, for example, an attitude to war
which the present generation, even allowing for what
we have seen of the horrible reality of human conflict
since those days when it still had its conventions, would
pronounce nonsense and blasphemy. Blackmore was
under no illusions about the carnage and suffering (there
is a graphic account in *The Maid of Sker,* of death and
mutilation in the Battle of the Nile), but it was, as
always, the way in which men were made and the
supreme test of patriotism and the personal courage
that was alone worthy of a woman's hand and heart:

> "Often had I longed for war, not from love of
> slaughter, but because it is so good for us. It calls
> out the strength of a man from his heart, into the
> swing of his legs and arms, and fills him with his
> duty to the land that is his mother; and scatters far
> away small things, and shows beyond dispute God's
> wisdom, when he made us male and female.
>
> The fair sex (after long peace) always want to take
> the lead of us, having rash faith in their quicker
> vigour of words and temper. But they prove their
> goodness always, coming down to their work at once,
> when the blood flows, and the bones are split into
> small splinters, and a man dies bravely in their arms,
> through doing his duty to them."

The robust conservatism of Blackmore, always im-
patient with fanatics and reformers, both political and
religious, is underlined in his crisp, satirical comments
on the idealists of the French Revolution:

"For they even went the length of declaring all men to be equal, the whole world common property, and the very names of the months all wrong! After this it was natural, and one might say the only sensible thing they ever did, to deny the existence of their maker. For it could hardly be argued that the Almighty ever did lay hand to such a lot of scoundrels."

So much for the foreigners, and as for the cranks who went about the English countryside proclaiming that the Second Advent was now obviously at hand, Blackmore had the words for them, too :

"Also all the lower lot of Nonconformists and schismatics ran with their tongues out, like mad dogs, all over the country raving, snapping at every good gentleman's heels, and yelping that the seventh vial was open, and the seventh seal broken. To argue with a gale of wind would show more sense than to try discussion with such a set of ninnies; and when I asked them to reconcile their admiration of atheism with their religious fervour, one of them answered bravely that he would rather worship the Goddess of Reason than the God of the Church of England."

Some pleasant descriptions of the region of Braunton Burrows brighten the early parts of the book, and there is undeniable vigour in the account of the naval engagements; but never are we convinced, as by *Lorna Doone,* that Blackmore had the time and the place and the loved one all together, and knew precisely how and what to tell us about them. Indeed, the "love interest" in *The Maid of Sker* is so slight that this fact, with a complaint about old Davy's extreme garrulousness, was the burden of the criticism in "The Saturday Review". The reviewer, while declaring that the book had "its merits and beauties", feared that "this lack will not tend to its popularity". When *The Maid of Sker* appeared in three volumes, after running as a serial in "Blackwood" from August, 1871, to April, 1872, the fear proved correct. The patrons of the circulating libraries much preferred Ouida and Miss Braddon.

VI

OCCASIONALLY there were visitors at Gomer House, and Blackmore was always very cordial in his invitations to the few whose friendship he sincerely valued. He preferred that such friends should come to him rather than he to them. The life of literary London did not interest him, and the kind of parties that were going on at Strawberry Hill, only a mile away in Horace Walpole's old house, he abhorred.

Sometimes Blackmore went over to see Sir Richard Owen, the great anatomist, who for his services as Lecturer in Natural History to the Royal Family and to science generally, had been presented with a house in Richmond Park. Sir Richard was a jealous and egoistic man, with an unalterable conviction that on any scientific point at issue he was right. In the controversy about evolution he had denounced Darwin as a pretentious amateur and had quarelled bitterly with his former pupil, Thomas Henry Huxley. His great-grandson has said that "he was a dominating and masterful spirit with great personal charm, which he could turn on and off like a tap".[1] The tap must have been usually turned on for Blackmore, as the novelist became very fond of him; probably there was something in Owen's blunt and downright manner which appealed to Blackmore, who was an outspoken person himself and not without his strong prejudices. When Owen and other friends pro-

[1] *The House in the Park* by F. D. Ommanney.

71

posed to come to Teddington, Blackmore always hoped
that they would not select a Saturday, as this was the
day on which he paid his staff. Normally he employed
ten gardeners, at the rate of three shillings a day. There
were also occasional visits to Mortimer Collins, a minor
novelist and poet, at Knowl Hill, near Wargrave. Collins
dedicated one of his novels, called *The Vivian Romance*
(published in 1870) to "Richard Doddridge Blackmore,
Poet and Gardener"; a gesture which somewhat annoyed
Blackmore, who disliked the appellation and had not
been allowed to read the book first.

In the year 1875 a meeting of great interest took place
in Blackmore's home. Thomas Hardy came over from
Surbiton to see him. Hardy, then 35 years of age, was
writing *The Hand of Ethelberta,* which proved as disappointing to admirers of *Far from the Madding Crowd*
as *The Maid of Sker* to the ever-growing multitudes who
loved *Lorna Doone.* Hardy and Blackmore had both
spent their young days in a remote countryside, and
both had now achieved some reputation as exponents
of the pastoral novel. They were united in a love for
customs and traditions that were passing away; both had
ears that could catch, and be delighted by, the cadences
of old songs that sprang from the heart of the people.
Both had a deep respect for men of action, and especially for the great English heroes of the early nineteenth
century. Blackmore and Hardy shared, too, an affection
for Greek and Latin classical literature, the latter, with
none of the educational advantages enjoyed by the former, having had to a great extent to find his own way

towards a reasonable proficiency in both languages. But between the two men there was a great gulf fixed; and it was made by the vast difference in their outlook on life.

The religious storms of the middle years of the nineteenth century, which seemed to some at that time to have destroyed the belief in the importance of human beings in the scheme of the universe, had confirmed Hardy's own growing conviction that man's hopes and fears counted as nothing in the end in a world which bore no certain marks of a loving and intelligent purpose. He turned with enthusiasm to the writings of the scientific materialists, and came to believe that the Church was not anxious to bless and encourage the seeking mind. Emotionally he felt still attracted to the Church of his fathers and his youth, but intellectually he had abandoned its creeds. Charles Kingsley had said that Christians now had "to choose between the absolute empire of accident and a living, immanent, ever-working God". Hardy had chosen the one, and Blackmore the other. Blackmore, seven years after the publication of *The Origin of Species,* cried out, in *Cradock Nowell,* his own deep and unchangeable faith: "Do what we will, and think as we may, enlarging the mind in each generation, growing contemptuous of contempt, casting caste to the winds of heaven, and antiquating prejudice, nevertheless shall we ever outrun or overtake true Christianity? Science, learning, philosophy, may regard it through a telescope: they touch it no more than astronomy sets foot upon a star . . . Of all the creeds which have issued as yet from God, or man, or the devil, is there another so far in advance of human civilization? True Christianity, like hope, cheers us to continual effort, exalts us to unbounded prospect, flies in front of our best success. Let us call it a worn-out garb, when we have begun to wear it; as yet the mantle is in the skies, and we have only the skirt with the name on it". Hardy, who was later to sneer violently against Browning's "smug Christian optimism", would no doubt have made the same comments about Blackmore's robust, personal religion. If they touched on these subjects in their conversation, we may perhaps assume that Hardy left Gomer House with a certain envy of such assurance in a region where he could not follow.

Blackmore was forced to take longer over the writing of his next novel than was customary with him, because of an accumulation of domestic difficulties and personal handicaps. He could not get a satisfactory servant, and had threats of his old epileptic malady. His wife was delicate, and he gave much time to assisting her in the house; and there was the constant battle in the garden against pests, early and late frosts, and fruit-loving birds. More delay followed when the work had reached the proofs stage, for publication in three volumes after running as a serial in "Blackwood". The publisher's "corrector" greatly irritated Blackmore by challenging the historical accuracy of certain statements about the Napoleonic wars and the correctness of certain expressions made by one of the characters, forcing the author to point out in detail where the "corrector" was himself in error.

A modern critic has declared that *Alice Lorraine* "displays a remarkable poverty of incident, vitality, gusto, and dramatic motive".[1] But Blackmore, always a stern critic of his own work, thought very highly of it, and Professor J. W. Mackail declared in 1925 that it was his best book after *Lorna Doone*. The novel's chief attractions are in two or three of its characters and in some descriptive passages which again reveal Blackmore's fine art and knowledge welded in an appraisal of the rural scene. The story itself, set partly in Kentish orchards and partly in the South Downs country near Steyning, with an interlude in Spain, moves slowly, and for a long way the reader must feel that the author ought to obey the injunction of his own reflections in Chapter 30, that "it is high time to work, to strengthen the threads of the wavering plan, to tighten the mesh of the woven web, to cast about here and there for completion."

There is a loving and lively picture of the Rev. Struan Hales, the sporting Rector of West Lorraine, and a convincing description of some of the trials and triumphs of the British troops in Spain after Salamanca. Hilary, the central character of the story, here becomes involved with two Spanish nurses, and all but marries the designing one. The letters from home, seeking to restrain him, are remarkable examples of the Victorian attitude towards

---

[1] *Victorian Wallflowers,* by Malcolm Elwin.

"foreigners". Hilary's sister Alice seems destined by family pressure to marriage with a Captain Chapman whom she cordially dislikes, but is saved "from the saddest doom that can befall proud woman—wedlock with an object", by the discovery of an astrologer's ancient treasure. The best chapters in the book are the last dozen. They contain a magnificent description of the severe winter of 1813, "remarkable not only for perpetual frost, but for continual snowfall", as it affected the inhabitants of the little village beneath the Sussex Downs. Here one notes again Blackmore's power of observation, his skill in the description of the behaviour of natural phenomena so that the reader can enter fully into the experience. See, for instance, how carefully and convincingly he describes the beginning of the great blizzard, after building up, in the way Dickens loved to do, the contrast between the warmth of cosy, firelit rooms, and a desolate world with a "dense grey canopy of gathering snow-vapour" outside :

> "The snow began about seven o'clock, when the influence of the sun was lost; and for three days and three nights it snowed, without taking or giving breathing-time. It came down without any wind, or unfair attempt at drifting. The meaning of the sky was to snow and no more, and let the wind wait his time afterwards. There was no such thing as any spying between the flakes at any time. The flakes were not so very large, but they came as close together as the sand pouring down in an hour-glass. They never danced up and down, like gnats or motes, as common snowflakes do, but one on the

back of another fell, expecting millions after them. And if any man looked up to see that gravelly infinitude of pelting spots, which swarms all the air in a snowstorm, he might just as well have shut both eyes, before it was done by snowflakes."

For such felicities a modern reader may feel that the slow and roundabout journey he is taken in *Alice Lorraine* is worth while. But at the end, having caught no memorable glimpse of Alice herself through her creator's insistence on her demureness, innocence, and nobility, it is doubtful if he will agree with the opinion of the reviewer in "The Saturday Review," that she is "a model to the last of the purest and finest type of English girlhood."

Blackmore began his next novel as the last quarter of the century was reached, and finished it in the year in which Queen Victoria was proclaimed Empress of India, a symbolical prelude to British expansion which was to add to the Empire territories covering nearly five million square miles. By the opening of this period the Trade Union movement was in a highly prosperous condition, even the farm-labourers, largely untouched before 1872 by the improvements gained for the working-classes, having now secured, for at least a few years, an increase in their wages. In literature Thomas Hardy had sung "the dawn chorus" of his Wessex worthies in *Under the Greenwood Tree,* and had followed this with *Far from the Madding Crowd.* Blackmore's novels, from now on, contain numerous glancing references to the new movements astir in a world from which he felt himself estranged by his innate conservatism. "Moreover, he had what most folk now, of the very best kind, have almost outlived, a staunch and steadfast faith in the management of the world by its Maker. We are too clever now for all this, of course. But it must be allowed that this fine old faith bred courage, truth, and comfort." These words, spoken of Squire Oglander, are characteristic of the manner in which Blackmore passed judgment on the trends in politics and philosophy that displeased him.

Although this next novel, *Cripps the Carrier,* had no particular success, it is a good example of the field in which Blackmore's best work was done—the small, self-contained community of the English village in the 18th or early 19th century, with a number of outstanding "characters," living their tranquil lives against the background of Nature lovely in herself and magnificent in her constant witness to God-given laws.

Sub-titled "A Woodland Tale," *Cripps the Carrier* is set in the village of Beckley, a few miles north-east of Oxford, and now within easy reach of the tentacles of Headington's "development." It was an area which Blackmore knew well and, with benefit to his tale, he does not move outside it. The plot, hinging upon the disappearance of the Squire's daughter, is thin enough, and there are fewer than usual of Blackmore's rhapsodies upon the seasons, but the book does something to disprove the general notion that he was "an artist of externals, not of psychological nuances."[1] The character

[1] Sherard Vines: 100 *years of English Literature.*

of Zacchary Cripps is finely observed, and the chief
people in the little community, with their simple beliefs
and sometimes exasperating superstitions, are drawn with
a care for detail that gives the romance the stamp of
verisimilitude. Glimpses of local events, such as the May
Day singing of choristers from the tower of Magdalen
College and a cricket match between Islip and Beckley,
assist the impression of sunlight always too strong for
the dark plans and deeds of men to be concealed. Destiny
in this village, in strong contrast to what it is generally
doing in Hardy's Wessex, is working always towards the
triumph of a simple and persevering righteousness.

The unity of *Cripps the Carrier* is surprising in view
of the fact that Blackmore had even more interruptions
and even more prolonged absences from his study when
he was writing it, than had been the case with *Alice
Lorraine*. Writing to his friend Mrs. Alfred Hunt (the
wife of a landscape artist of some note in his day) on
February 21st 1876 he says:

> "Bad is my luck. For ten days now I have been
> laid up with most vile bronchitis, and cough which
> lets me neither eat nor sleep. I am not allowed to go
> out of doors, and ought to stay in bed, but won't.
> Just in the very crisis of my 'Cripps,' I cannot write
> one word.
> He has been the most unlucky fellow throughout,
> but this I fear will beat him. After long weeks I got
> rid of 'rheumatics,' but found no use of arm or hand.
> It is, the Doctor says, a little touch of paralysis of
> the left side. The hearing of the left ear is gone.
> However, why trouble you with these things?

Troubles enough has each mortal of her own. No one in the world can be better minded and looked after."

A month later, on March 23rd, he writes to Mrs. Hunt again :

"It is very hard upon me that I cannot come to see beautiful things and enjoy great kindness. But so it is. My vile rheumatism, and slight paralysis of left side passed into the worst Bronchial attack I ever had, and for nearly two months I have been altogether a prisoner. During all that time I have not even seen my own green-houses and everything is sure to be going wrong. Moreover I have tired the parish with my coughs, and am as stupid as a muting owl . . . "

Nevertheless, the work which emerged from this unhappy period achieved a number of new editions in the years that followed, and it is certainly among the half-dozen novels of Blackmore that ought to be rescued from the oblivion into which they have undeservedly fallen.

VII

AMONG Blackmore's regular correspondents were a number of Americans, who had greatly admired *Lorna Doone* and wrote to tell him so. Some of them visited him at Teddington, and with several he afterwards exchanged letters (and cuttings for the garden) for a considerable period. Blackmore was particularly attached to an American poet, Paul Hamilton Hayne, and the letters from one to the other that appear in Dr. Burris's dissertation[1] reveal the depth of their mutual affection. The simplicity and cordiality of the Americans he had known appealed to Blackmore strongly. So it was that for his next novel, partly to pay his friends a compliment and partly also to "stretch" himself as a writer in the great spaces and vast distances so much in contrast to the little countries of southern England, Blackmore chose the setting of California. The book was dedicated to "Artemise Talley, my little godchild in Kansas City."

The failure of *Erema* to please the reviewers or to attract readers was a bitter disappointment to its author, who called it his "most unlucky book." In it Blackmore reverted to the autobiographical method, and we first meet the girl Erema who tells the tale, as a young child in company with her father, emerging from an agonising desert to see ahead of them the fertile promise of California. But for the father it is too late. Worn out by sickness and the strain of much travelling in harsh

[1] *R. D. Blackmore,* by Q. Y. Burris.

81

F

regions, he dies in his daughter's arms. The girl subsequently falls in with a kindly family of sawyers, of whom the founder had been an emigrant Cornishman. Blackmore's tales sometimes remind one of the joke about the publisher who declared that the many novels of a best-selling author on his list had one thing in common—the same plot. It is all here, in the prose counterpart of innumerable Victorian paintings—the father wrongfully accused of another's crime, the prolonged searching of legal documents, the "just retribution," the "faithful and soft-hearted nurse" of childhood, the revelation that little Erema is mistress of the great estates of Castlewood—the library subscribers knew the whole mixture and were becoming allergic to it. In many, distaste must have been intensified by the sympathies Blackmore expresses for the cause of "the noble South" in the American Civil War. It was typical of the spiritual myopia with which so many Victorians were afflicted in the sphere of the ethical implications of their religion, that Blackmore should declare, in a letter to Paul Hamilton Hayne, that "the outcry against 'Slavery' has always seemed to me a sample of ignorant clap-trap, such as makes hideous this British air." In another letter to the same correspondent, he is indignant because "the blessed Nigger . . . seems to be a horrible pest among you, & destroys your tranquillity." *Erema* moves for several chapters to "Bruntsea," and gives us some pleasant glimpses of the country around Rye, Sussex. Many Americans who read the story in the pages of "Harper's Magazine" probably found satisfaction in the description

of Californian scenes done by a man who had never left
the shores of his native country. But the book as a whole
leaves one wondering how it could have been written
by the same hand that created *Lorna Doone*. And once
again for Blackmore chagrin was added to disappointment, because the reviewers had charged him "with
their own blunders."

Blackmore, grumbling to his friends about the
weather, his own maladies, the shortcomings of servants,
the wicked practices of wholesale fruit-merchants, the
noise of the railway that had come to the bottom of his
garden, and the inconsiderateness of "anti-enclosure"
agitators, often does not appear from his letters to be
the person of sweetness and light to whom we are presented by those who have left memories of him. But constantly and genuinely he recognised his own faults and
scolded himself for them, and against his prejudices and
his occasional aggressiveness we may set his humility and
his entire absence of self-conceit. His integrity, arising
from his steady vision of the eternal verities, makes him
in personal principles probably the finest of all the notable Victorian writers.

Often, in spite of the varied types he loved to draw,
he appeared to be more in love with places than with
people, and he had a rare power of projecting himself
into a locality which appealed to him as the right setting
for a story that was already unfolding as he looked at
it. He was always wanting to explore the characteristics
of new regions. In the late summer of 1877 he and Mrs.
Blackmore (who had been much ailing during the year)

went off to the Whitby area of Yorkshire for a holiday. Blackmore was uplifted by the healthy breezes of the bare and jagged coast, and charmed by the wild countryside behind it, with lanes as pretty "as may anywhere be found in any other county than that of Devon." It did not take him long to discover in these wide acres a pleasant farm, "not so large or rambling as to tire the mind or foot, yet wide enough and full of change—rich pasture, hazel copse, green valleys, fallows brown, and golden breastlands pillowing into nooks of fern, clumps of shade for horse or heifer, and for rabbits sandy warrens, furzy cleve for hare and partridge, not without a little mere for willows and for wild ducks." Over it ruled Stephen Annerley, "a thrifty and well-to-do Yorkshire farmer of the olden type . . . Happy alike in the place of his birth, his lot in life, and the wisdom of the powers appointed over him, he looked up, with a substantial faith, yet a solid reserve of judgment, to the Church, the Justices of the Peace, spiritual lords and temporal, and above all His Majesty George the Third." And of course in the farmhouse is the girl of Blackmore's dreams, very similar to all his other maidens in idyllic bowers, but sharing with Clara Vaughan a certain headstrong wilfulness which at least removes her a shade from impossible perfection.

Another of Blackmore's parsons makes his appearance in the person of the Rev. Turner Upround, Rector of Hamborough. "Happy in a pleasant nature, kindly heart, and tranquil home, he was also happy in those awards of life in which men are helpless." He represents

Blackmore's own ideal of the pastor in parochia and is drawn with the admiration his creator always felt for sound godliness in a sensible and balanced personality. "Such a man generally thrives in the thriving of his flock and does not harry them. He gives them spiritual food enough to support them without daintiness, and he keeps the proper distinction between the Sunday and the poorer days. He clangs no bell of reproach upon a Monday, when the squire is leading the lady in to dinner, and the labourer sniffing at his supper-pot, and he lets the world play on a Saturday, while he works his own head to find good words for the morrow. Because he is a wise man who knows what other men are, and how seldom they desire to be told the same thing, more than a hundred and four times in the year." Into the story comes a handsome smuggler, cast up (like Bardie in *The Maid of Sker*) by the waves, who eventually redeems himself at the battle of Trafalgar, in which he is close to Nelson ("one of the noblest men that ever lived upon the tide of time"), is discovered to be the son of the wealthy landowner Sir Duncan Yordas, and proves a worthy winner of Mary's heart and hand.

Mary Anerley must rank high in the list of Blackmore's novels. It shows an unaccustomed discipline in its creator's unfolding of the plot, has many witty comments on human frailties, and minor characters who are credible and sometimes memorable. The Yorkshireman (A. J. Munby, a Barrister-at-Law) to whom, "owing much to his kind aid," is was dedicated, must have felt it thoroughly deserving of warm acceptance. Once more, however, it is in his description of the changing moods of earth and sky and sea, and the crispness of his observation of little, secret things (a crispness coming unexpectedly at times on the heels of a particularly involved passage) that Blackmore "finds" us. Examples in *Mary Anerley* are the beautifully etched picture of the vast and sudden activity in Hamborough when the mackerel arrive in the bay, and the vignette of a corner of the farm on a warm day in August. "There was not a horse standing down by a pool, with his stiff legs shut up into biped form, nor a cow staring blandly across an old rail, nor a sheep with a pectoral cough behind a hedge, not a rabbit making rustle at the eyebrow of his hole . . . " Twenty years earlier, Blackmore, noting the same scene, would have felt that it needed a page to convey it to the reader.

Blackmore was now 57, and at an age when a novelist's best work is generally presumed to be behind him. The years ahead were to be difficult ones, made so by the vast shadow that was to fall over his life and labours in the passing of his wife, his own beloved "Lorna," by personal and increasing ill-health, and by his continued failure to make an impact on the great public who had *Lorna Doone,* and were content to regard him as a man who had made one masterpiece and could never achieve another. But Blackmore, though much less prolific than Trollope with his sixty novels and Thackeray with the great mass of his contributions to periodical literature, as well as his outstanding works, had, like both of these, the constant urge to write about a world that was real to him. This world was "sharply divided between good and bad . . . For the purposes of romance, Blackmore must have such a world, and have it he did. The force of love he made operative in simple people of the landed yeoman class; people lowly, faithful, honest, of clean lives, strong and sturdy masculinity, solidity of character, kindliness, and tolerance of human foibles so long as they were not base. These people, wrought upon by love, he set down in rustic places, beyond the artificiality of metropolitan life, in places of natural beauty such as he himself loved, and such as were fitted to reflect the glamour of their love-time and the storm of anguish to which they were sometimes subjected."[1]

The study of country life and character produced in the closing years of the century some works which have never lacked delighted readers in successive generations, despite the ever-increasing range of the novel in the past seventy years. Besides Thomas Hardy there were Richard Jefferies, W. H. Hudson, Eden Philpotts, A. T. Quiller-Couch, and George Macdonald; all these moved in regions unaffected by the rapid developments in thought and invention which marked the period. Richard Jefferies was staying on Exmoor in the summer of 1882, the year in which Blackmore's next novel was published. The literary fruit of the visit was *Red Deer* and several essays on the Somerset countryside, and if Blackmore read Jefferies he would have approved the latter's careful and affectionate delineation of Exmoor's beauty. Certainly Jefferies had read *Lorna Doone,* for

[1] *Blackmore,* by Quincy Guy Burris.

he refers in his essays to the tradition behind the exploits of Tom Faggus.

Christowell, set a little south of the Christow which gave Blackmore some features of the story, and while only "five leagues off from the dark square towers of Exeter Cathedral," yet "as remote from a day as the central sahara", is simply "A Dartmoor Tale." A mile from the village, under a jagged tor, stood a lonely cottage whose solitary occupant had helped the hand of nature to secure his quietude. This person, known to the village as "Captain Larks," is the most firmly-drawn and convincing character in the book, largely because while he was being drawn Blackmore was looking at himself in a mirror. The curiosity of the villagers in a little place "where everybody knows, twice a day, how everybody else's cough is; and scarcely can the most industrious woman find anything to say, that she has not said thrice," and the reserve of the "Captain," who had come out of another world and wanted only to be left alone to cultivate his fertile garden, gave Blackmore ample scope for sly reflections on human peculiarities and for good advertisement of his accurate knowledge of the Devonshire dialect. There is some fine prose in *Christowell,* and nowhere is Blackmore's nature-realism seen to greater advantage than in his magnificent account of the storm which accounts for the villain and passes into a horrifying memory handed on from one generation to another. Blackmore got the idea of the storm, and certainly some of the details, from the calamity which struck the church at Widecombe-in-the-

Moor in October, 1638. This killed four people and injured sixty-two; at Christowell on a Sunday afternoon during divine service seven perished and sixty-two were injured, "but not a single child was hurt."

> "They were singing the psalm before the sermon, with an unusual depth of voice; encouraging one another's vitality, as they do at funerals. Each man, with his open mouth, nudged up to his neighbour growing dark to him; and the women in the lower row, held hands, to keep their voices. A peculiar smell oppressed the church; as if the dead were rising.
>
> The great west door, beneath the tower, was open, where the bell-ropes hung, with the frayed hemp glistening in the darkness, like so many hangman's nooses. Gaston stole his way between them, to the pillar of the western arch; and slipped into the church unseen; for every mind was overborne with a heavy load of doubt and fear; and every eye was cowering, at the creeping shades of roof and wall.
>
> The cold awe of the vaulted gloom redoubled Gaston's terror; and he sank upon a low bench fitted round the octagonal plinth of a tall, gray pier. Then he pulled off his flexible hat, and muttered some confused words into it; and if they were not words of prayer, it was from want of practice.
>
> The vicar, with a slow and solemn step, went up the winding pulpit-stairs, every rustle of his surplice sounding, through the breathless hush around. And when he knelt, for his own silent prayer upon the cushion, the murmuring of the Christow brook came in at the chancel window, and was heard throughout the church by many, who had never heard it there before, and never should hear it anywhere again.

THE LAST VICTORIAN

The parson's voice was trembling slightly, not from fear, but solemn awe, as he pronounced his text, the prayer of David in the hour of dread—*Let me fall into the hand of the Lord*. Before he had pronounced it twice, thick blackness fell upon roof, and window, pillar, arch, and sepulchral stone . . A man could scarcely see his wife, or little ones, at his elbow; mothers caught their children up, to be sure of being near them; and the preacher's voice came out of the night . . .

Then fell the greatest crash of tempest ever known in England. The tower was cleft, the church was rent, the people cast, like blasted straws. The roof flew wide, the pillars snapped, the timbers fell like cobwebs, and the walls were riven as a bladder bursts. Pitchy night, and stifling vapour, shrouded all who were unconsumed . . .

All, who got over it, are agreed that it must have gone on, for at least five minutes; and some say a great deal more than that. It began, with a great ball of fire descending, and splitting the north side of the tower, then scorching all the bell-ropes, and passing up the nave, after killing one man in the archway. Then it killed another man, with his head against a stone, by driving his skull into the granite, took all the hair off an elderly woman (her Sunday hair, new that morning), and then parted into a big globe, and a small one; the big going out through the roof, and the small one through the chancel window.

After that, nobody knows what happened; for they all fell down upon their faces, with the thundering of stones and beams above them, and conviction of the Judgement-day. In the stench of sulphur, men held breath, and women chewed their

90

handkerchiefs. Through the woodwork of the pews, they could see the lightning to and fro, like clotted snakes; and a roar (like an overshot wheel in a flood) rang along their backbones."

Christowell has another claim on the modern reader's interest, in its glimpses of the happy simplicity of village life at the beginning of the reign of Queen Victoria. Blackmore was wrong in his criticism of certain aspects of the contemporary scene, but profoundly right in others. He knew something about the compensations offered in "the quiet runs of shadow, where poor people live and are content." He knew that shepherds and woodmen are "giant symbols of everlasting truth," and that the seasonal rejoicings, made from the intertwining of Christian and pagan beliefs, of these small communities, came spontaneously from man's poetic and truth-finding imagination. So in *Christowell* we glance back at little Moreton Hampstead, when the ancient elm stood by the village cross, and was known as the "Dancing Tree," because of the May Day frolics that went on around it. High up in the tree was built a wooden platform to which the most venturesome young lasses climbed by means of a ladder, while the lads had to get up to them by means of "a half-inch rope, hanging down from a bough, and anointed well with mutton-suet." And in the wide and lovely moorland there is reaping-day and harvest supper, and at Okehampton the day's great event comes when the coach from Falmouth stops at the "White Hart"; while in Moreton Hampstead the cry of the "window-washing boy" breaks the silence of summer morning. 91

VIII

Shut away from the world as securely as "Captain Larks", Blackmore was yet aware of uprisings and movements and prophetic voices in the Victorian heyday which presaged the vast changes in social conditions and customs that were soon to come. In the early 'eighties English socialism was born again to a fresh and significant vigour. A year before the publication of *Christowell,* H. M. Hyndman, who in 1881 had produced *England for All* (an appeal to the nations to face the questions involved in the poverty of millions of workers and the rise of democracy), published his *Historic Basis of Socialism,* which introduced the ideas of Karl Marx to the English-speaking world. In 1885 William Morris, with Belfort Bax and Edward Aveling, formed the Socialist League; the Fabian Society had been founded a year earlier. Technical education was being improved to meet the challenge from the Continent, and especially from Germany; and scientific method employed in regions which people did not customarily talk about. A prosecution in 1877 had even given publicity to the practical details of birth-control.

Blackmore knew what was going on, and he did not like it. He resolved on "an extravaganza upon the Glads., Rads., and Sads.", an "amusing" and "facetious" story directed chiefly against "the pugnacious Socialists" and the "Scientists". The result was the publication in 1884

93

of *The Remarkable History of Sir Thomas Upmore,
Bart., M.P., formerly known as "Tommy Upmore"*.

No doubt it gave Blackmore a certain satisfaction to
be able to snipe at the enemy from the seclusion of his
orchards, but this is about all it achieved. It is a little
difficult to believe that even those who have come to
know, in Professor Dunn's words, "the strong likes and
dislikes of the author," and take up the book armed with
such knowledge, "will have a delightful experience, and
leave it with a still warmer feeling for its author." The
satire is mainly of the clumsy and obvious kind :

> The first need of all was to get rid of landowners.
> Land belongs to every one, and therefore to no one.
> Why have men got feet, except to plant them where
> they like? Nature has implanted in the human heart
> a profound desire for the ownership of land. This
> proves that everybody must own land. But how,
> without kicking every other body out? Towards that,
> the first step is to kick out present owners. When the
> others get in, they must be kicked out too . . . "

The garment of satire was not really becoming to
Blackmore, and he might have done well to heed his
own words about it in *Lorna Doone* : "For it strikes me
that of all human dealings, satire is the very lowest, and
most mean and common. It is the equivalent in words,
for what bullying is in deeds; and no more bespeaks a
clever man, than the other does a brave one . . . And
though a good man may commit the one fault or the
other, now and then, by way of outlet, he is sure to

have compunctions soon, and to scorn himself more than the sufferer." One is forced again to remark the astonishing paradoxes of the age. Blackmore, with his deep appreciation of the things that enrich human life, his personal kindliness, his power of sympathy with humble folk in remote places, and comfortable enough within the eleven acres that had come to him by the inheritance of money, yet protests against the "pugnacity" of Socialists at a time when the dock-labourers were demanding a minimum wage of *sixpence* an hour.

Having in this way made his protest at what he conceived to be a sorry chapter in English history, but under no delusion that it was merely a passing phase before common sense reasserted itself, Blackmore turned back to some of the pages that never failed to inspire him with proud and deeply patriotic sentiments. These pages were dominated by the conquering heroes, waging their holy wars in defence of English freedom or for the extension of English interests; and of all these perhaps Nelson commanded his greatest veneration. The annals of the Napoleonic wars had cast a spell upon Blackmore since childhood, as had been the case with Thomas Hardy, who in 1880 had produced *The Trumpet-Major*, and ten years after *Springhaven* was to begin work on *The Dynasts*. But in how different a mood and with what different intent Hardy came to his great work of philosophical musing on the fateful workings of the Immanent Will "as a brainlike network of currents and ejections, twitching, interpenetrating, entangling and thrusting hither and thither the human forms." The

events of those days were for Blackmore signal examples
of Divine Providence and Judgment; the notion that the
whole scheme of world domination planned by the
Emperor of the French might, by some inexplicable
quirk of the Immanent Will, have come to such fruition,
would have seemed to him blasphemous and absurd.
Whatever the delays and temporary thwartings of His
plan, God always vindicated the righteous and produced
"the man for the moment." "It is an old saying that
nature has provided for every disease its remedy, and
challenges men to find it out, which they are clever
enough not to do. For that deadly disease Napoleon,
the remedy was Nelson; and as soon as he should be
consumed, another would appear in Wellington."

Sir Walter Scott had begun, in the years around
Waterloo, to give the historical novel a new stature and
importance in the literary scene, so that the forty years
between *Waverley* and *Westward Ho!* may be described
as being, through the influence of the man ranked by
Walt Whitman as "next to Shakespeare," its "Golden
Age". The historical novel made occasional appearances
after 1855 (witness Charles Reade's *The Cloister and
the Hearth* and Dickens's *A Tale of Two Cities*), but
the second half of the nineteenth century has few outstanding examples of the type to offer. When it began
a new era of popularity with R. L. Stevenson, it flourished also in the hands of Stanley Weyman, Conan
Doyle, and others, mainly in the "cloak-and-dagger"
form, and has continued ever since to provide us not
only with historical "romances" which are concerned

more with adventure than with strict accuracy, but also with outstanding books which, making use of the great new field of historical knowledge now open to us, give us careful and genuine pictures of the past.

Blackmore chose as the period of his new novel, the opening years of the nineteenth century, when Napoleon, in his scheme for reorganising Europe as a commonwealth under French hegemony, planned to begin it with the invasion and conquest of England. Here he expected to find an oppressed population eager to shake off the tyrranous yoke of George III, and ready to welcome the setting-up of the republic which the conqueror would offer. For two years a great force of French soldiers waited along the coast for an invasion order that never came. Nelson and Cornwallis watched the French and Spanish fleets, ready to attack with superior numbers whenever the moment arrived; and the invasion project was finally shattered with the victory of Trafalgar. Yet while the life of the great country-houses went on happily and jovially, the danger existed and the threat loomed large in the lives of many people along our southern and eastern coasts before that memorable day; and it was upon a small community in Sussex, close to Hastings with its record of a successful invader who had landed there nearly eight hundred years earlier and changed our history, that Blackmore focused his interest in those tense and exciting days "when England trusted mainly to the vigour and valour of one man, against a world of enemies."

"Springhaven" is Newhaven, then a quiet little fishing

village in a tranquil Sussex valley, and, according to Blackmore's Nelson, "the place of all places in England for the French to land." To Springhaven came one Caryl Carne, to store French arms in the vaults of his ancestors' disintegrating castle and to seek to dissuade local folk from their allegiance to their king. One of his special targets in this connection was Dolly Darling, daughter of Admiral Charles Darling and god-daughter of Lord Nelson, who was an old friend of the family. Dan Tugwell, deceived by Carne, allowed himself to be made the pilot of a ship engaged in carrying French arms to the castle, and Grocer Cheeseman, entangled in Carne's net through intimidation, was forced to hand over a small vessel, "The London Trader", to be used for the same purpose. While all this plotting was going on, Nelson came down to Springhaven to warn Admiral Darling of the possibility of an invasion; accordingly a local defence force of all sorts and conditions of men was mustered, and George III himself came down to review these amateur troops on the Downs behind the village, as he had travelled to Weymouth for the same purpose in *The Trumpet Major*. Into the picture also comes Blyth Scudamore, a young naval lieutenant, formerly a schoolmaster, whose somewhat priggish but good-hearted character is modelled on that of one of Blackmore's early friends who became a missionary in Africa and had the same surname. Blyth, who loved Dolly Darling, was captured in a naval action off the French coast, but while talking a walk on parole over-heard Carne discussing with Napoleon the projected invasion. Blyth thereupon managed to escape from captivity, and got back to Springhaven, where he found that Dolly, at last awake to Carne's real intentions, had refused to hand over to him some important papers sent to her father. With his treachery now exposed Carne decided to blow up his castle and flee to France, but his plans miscarried. A stumble in the munition-filled cellars prevented him from getting away in time as he lighted the fuse to his stored gunpowder, and his end was as violent and dramatic as Carver Doone's on Exmoor and George Gaston's in *Christowell*. The last chapters bring all to a happy conclusion. Blyth marries Dolly, and at the Battle of Trafalgar it is the hand of Dan Tugwell which despatches the Frenchman who had deprived the world of Nelson.

In Caryl Carne Blackmore has drawn a rather more credible character than most of his other villains, and the spell he casts over Dolly is one that is fully understandable in the light of the psychological make-up of the man and the girl; Blackmore took more pains with his creation of both of them than was usual with him. Strongly noticeable, too, in this book is his sense of *compassion* for all human creatures; he had something of that "vast universal charity" which is the greatness of Dickens and Dostoevsky and always the mark of the greatest writers. However contemptuous of his rogues and however strongly he underlined their sheer and abominable wickness, one always detects in Blackmore's attitude to them this note of infinite pity; for the purpose in the heart of the Person who made the world is not the destruction of evil, but its redemption. One is reminded of Charles Lamb's sorrowing description of Matravis: "Nothing that is great, nothing that is amiable, existed for this unhappy man. He feared, he envied, he suspected; but he never loved. The Sublime and Beautiful in Nature, the Excellent and Becoming in Morals, were things placed beyond the capacity of his sensations. He loved not Poetry—nor ever took a lonely walk to meditate—never beheld Virtue, which he did not try to disbelieve, or Female Beauty and Innocence, which he did not lust to contaminate." The inevitable parson in the book is the the Rev. Joshua Twemlow, "no prig, no pedant, and no popinjay, but a sensible, upright honourable man, whose chief defect was a quick temper." When Lord Nelson came down to Spring-haven and announced his intention of going to church on the Sunday, Parson Twemlow had it in mind to include in his sermon some "leading truths in a general way, and let him make the home application." From this course the parson was dissuaded by his wife, who pointed out that Nelson had his own Rector at Merton, a Chaplain at sea, and a father and brother who were clergymen, and would probably not understand the reference in any case! Evidently Blackmore was not so lost in hero-worship as to be unconscious of those lapses from virtue on Nelson's part for which many condemned him; but he passes no judgment on the man, only on the nation for allowing the melancholy chapters that closed the story of Lady Hamilton.

Blackmore's delightful humour, by which *Spring-*

haven is frequently enriched, is seen in such shrewd and playful observations as he passes upon one of Parson Twemlow's pleasures :

> "He did not pretend to be a learned man, any more than he made any other pretence which he could not justify. But he loved a bit of Latin, whenever he could find anybody to share it with him, and even in lack of intelligent partners he indulged sometimes in that utterance. This was a grievance to the Squire of the parish, because he was expected to enjoy at ear-shot that which had passed out of the other ear in boyhood, with a painful echo behind it. But the Admiral had his revenge by passing the Rector's bits of Latin on—when he could remember them—to some one entitled to an explanation, which he, with a pleasant smile, vouchsafed. This is one of the many benefits of a classical education."

Blackmore took care with his historical portraits, and particularly in the case of Nelson, whom he thus sees as the great man comes down to watch the fishing fleet put into harbour and to give them some sound advice at the same time :

> "For although he was not in uniform, and bore no sword, his dress was conspicuous, as he liked to have it, and his looks and deeds kept suit with it. For he wore a blue coat (very badly made, with gilt buttons and lappets too big for him), a waistcoat of dove-coloured silk, very long, coming over the place where his stomach should have been, and white plush breeches, made while he was blockading Boulogne in 1801, and therefore had scarcely any

flesh upon his bones. Peace having fattened him a
little, these breeches had tightened upon him (as
their way is with a boy having six weeks' holiday);
but still they could not make his legs look big, though
they showed them sharp and muscular. Below them
were brisk little sinewy calves in white silk hose, with
a taper descent to ankles as fine as a lady's, and in-
steps bright with large silver buckles. Yet that which
surpassed all the beauty of the clothes was the vigour
of the man inside them, who seemed to animate the
whole with life, even to the right sleeve, doubled
up from the want of any arm inside it. But the loss
of the right arm, and the right eye also, seemed to
be of no account to the former owner, so hard did
he work with the residue of his body, and so much
did he express with it.

His noble cocked hat was in its leathern box yet,
for he was only just come from Merton; but the
broad felt he wore was looped up in front, and displayed all the power of his countenance, or rather
the vigour—for power is heavy—and his face was
light and quickness. Softness also, and a melancholy
gift of dreaminess and reflection, enlarged and impressed the effect of a gaze and a smile which have
conquered history."

He is a man utterly confident and entirely convinced
of his own brilliance as a naval tactician, and sometimes speaks in a way which would fill the average man,
who likes some modesty in his heroes, with keen distaste.
"If God Almighty prolongs my life—which is not very
likely—it will be that I may meet that scoundrel,
Napoleon Bonaparte, on dry land. I hear that he is eager
to encounter me on the waves, himself commanding a

line-of-battle ship. I should send him to the devil in a
quarter of an hour. And ashore I could astonish him, I
think, a little, if I had a good army to back me up.
Remember what I did at Bastia, in the land that produced this monster, and where I was called the Brigadier;
and again, upon the coast of Italy, I showed that I
understood all their dry-ground business."

Blackmore's skill as an observer and listener in obscure
corners of forgotten places, by which as a writer he is
specially distinguished, is often at work in this novel.
The reader will recognise at once, for example, the
fidelity of Blackmore's vision as he watches Carne riding
slowly back from Springhaven to his castle one summer
evening :

> "The beauty of the night had kept him back, for
> he hated to meet people on the road. The lingering
> gossips, the tired faggot-bearers, the youths going
> home from the hay-rick, the man with a gun who
> knows where the hares play, and beyond them all
> the truant sweethearts who cannot have enough of
> one another, and wish 'good-night' at every corner
> of the lane, till they tumble over one or other's
> cottage steps—all these to Caryl Carne were a smell
> to be avoided, an eye-sore to shut the eyes at. He
> let them get home, and pull their boots off, and get
> the frying-pan a bubbling—for they ended the day
> with a bit of bacon, whenever they could cash or
> credit it—and then he set forth upon his lonely ride,
> striking fear into the heart of any bad child that
> lay awake."

Not less compelling is the way in which Blackmore

portrays the shadow falling over the peace, the communication of the tension of those days of expectancy and of the sounds which echoed everlastingly in his own heart :

> "From point to point, and from height to height, like a sprinkle of blood, the red lights ran; and the roar of guns from the moonlit sea made echo that they were ready. Then the rub-a-dub-dub of the drum arose, and the thrilling blare of trumpet; the great deep of the night was heaved and broken with the stir of human storm; and the staunchest and strongest piece of earth—our England—was ready to defend herself."

Those who have lived through a similar moment in the history of Britain and tell their children of battles fought in the skies above the Kent and Sussex villages which Blackmore loved, will find in such words the grim and surging excitement of an old drama repeated in their own time. It must be added, for the benefit of the countless admirers of C. S. Forester's *Hornblower*, who have never heard of *Springhaven*, that they have missed a novel which has merits of plot, character-drawing, humour and narrative power that no other writer dealing with that period of our history has equalled.

It is pleasant to record that *Springhaven* had some success in its first printing, and later received the accolade of inclusion in the early volumes of "Everyman". When the book came out, Bernard Shaw was writing almost unnoticed novels in serial form for obscure periodicals; and the "best-seller" of that year was Fergus Hume's *The Mystery of a Hansom Cab*.

IX

On January 31st 1888, Lucy Blackmore, after many
years of suffering, died quietly from acute inflammation
of the lungs. Blackmore was as overwhelmed by grief at
this event after his thirty-six years of married life as
William Barnes had been by the departure of his Julia.
Barnes had poured his sorrow into one of his most moving poems, "Wife A-Lost."

> "Since I noo mwore do zee your feäce,
>   Up steäirs or down below,
> I'll zit me in the lwonesome pleäce
>   Where flat-bough'd beech do grow :
> Below the beeches' bough, my love,
>   Where you did never come,
> An' I don't look to meet ye now,
>   As I do look at hwome."

Blackmore wrote to his friend Hayne : "I seem to have
no idea where I am, and little concern to ask about it,
knowing only that what remains of life must be cold
and desolate." And to Mrs. Hunt : "I am lost in the
width of loneliness." Again and again in the twelve years
that remained to him Blackmore wrote of, or dwelt
sorrowfully upon, this saddest day of his life, as Barnes
in all the thirty-four years he was destined to face without his beloved, had been haunted through them all by
the picture of "the geäte a-vallin to."

Through the clouded spring and summer of that year

105

Blackmore wrote nothing, but with another autumn upon him he had a strong urge to pen some of his happiest memories of his own "love-time" in a new novel. The motive for the writing of *Kit and Kitty* was undoubtedly Blackmore's desire to recapture some of the bliss of his early days with his "Kitty," and to find some solace in the unfolding of a tale of love triumphant over adverse circumstance.

On the manuscript of the novel, written in his neat, minute hand on exercise books contained in a stiff binder, Blackmore has stated that he began it on October 1st and finished it on July 21st in the following year. One has an affecting picture of the childless widower, author of a book that by now had gone through thirty editions, wrapped more closely than ever in the solitude of a darkened house which he shared with a niece who came to look after him, troubled by arthritis and feeling that there could now remain for him only fitful gleams of sunshine; but still pursuing with his old hope and courage the two great interests of his life—the cultivation of his orchards and the craft of fiction.

It would be pleasant indeed to be able to record that out of this sorrowful time came a work of note and importance. But *Kit and Kitty* merely tells with fair competence a tale that many would judge scarcely worth the telling. Set chiefly in Sunbury, but touching also the Thames-side regions of Shepperton, Hampton, and Hanworth, it has none of those memorable descriptions of the countryside which are found so often in most of Blackmore's other books. There is sometimes a bathos worse even than the sudden descents of Thomas Hardy, and there are passages of fantastic sentimentality which would be joyfully plucked by someone looking for examples of Victorian fiction at its worst, such as those describing the reunion of the lover and his beloved, after a number of quite incredible mistakes and misunderstandings:

> "She was threatened with hysterics; but I soothed her gently, and she rested on my breast with her eyes half closed. As I looked at her, I felt that in this rapture I could die.
>
> 'Darling, I can hardly believe it yet;' she whispered, playing with my fingers to make sure; 'see, this is my wedding-ring, I never took it off. What fine gold it is, not to tarnish with my tears. The drops that have fallen on it—oh, I wonder there is any blue left in my eyes at all! Do you think they are as blue, dear, as when you used to love them?'
>
> 'They are bluer, heart of hearts. They are larger and deeper. The tears of true love have made them still more lovely.' "

Or the paragraph in which the villain seeks to take his revenge as he lies on the ground, a dying man:

> "Suddenly a red glare as of lightning filled his eyes, his features worked horribly, and his great teeth clashed as he tried to jerk me towards him. Luckily for me I was poised upon both feet. At the flash of his eyes, I sprang aside, a redder flash blinded me, and a roar rang in my ears, and upon the bosom of the dying man lay the short thick curl, the love-lock that Kitty was so fond of playing with. The ball

had passed within an inch of my temple, and my
forehead was black with the pistol-smoke."

The chief interest of the book is in the portrait of the
market-gardener, "Uncle Corny," for it is clearly in
many respects a portrait of Blackmore himself. For this
honest, rugged, and downright character, "few things
vexed him much, except to find his things sold below
their value; and that far less for the love of money than
from the sense of justice." "If ever there was a man who
gave good change for sixpence, ay, and took good care
to get it, too, you will own it was my Uncle Corny."

Uncle Corny, however, in contrast to Blackmore,
appears to have been a consistently successful grower.
Certainly he suffered at times from "the rogues in the
neighbourhood of Covent Garden," but when he was
wronged "he was not the man to make a to-do and
write to the papers about it. All he did was to drive his
stick into the floor, and look up at the ceiling." Blackmore himself showed no such restraint, and letters from
him, complaining at the poor prices received from the
wholesalers, appeared on a number of occasions in "The
Times."

Kit and Kitty will always have some special appeal
to those who know well the region of the Thames Valley
which is the scene of the story, and they will note with
interest Blackmore's references to such long-vanished
things as "the great wax-works at Teddington", and
"Woking Road Station." But Blackmore nowhere com-
municates the beauty of the neighbourhood at blossom-

time as vividly as George Meredith, nor the sombreness of the flat lands in autumn twilight as strikingly as Mrs. Riddell, who was writing about them in prolific fashion in this very year while living at Upper Halliford, near Shepperton.

The book had been produced under conditions of extreme difficulty, similar in some respects to those faced by Wilkie Collins when he dictated *The Moonstone* "in the intervals of grief, in the intermissions of pain." There was to be no change in the situation for Blackmore, despite the devoted attentions of his niece and the solace of occasional contact with a few warm friends; but he did not believe that the time had yet come for him to lay down his pen. His memory, straying back over his happiest "spring-bright" years, was held by a vision of the lovely corner of East Devon, at the foot of the Blackdowns, he had known as a boy. It was at Culmstock that his father had served as curate-in-charge, and from the Vicarage Blackmore had gone out many a time on a journey of solitary exploration.

Along the Culm Valley, distant less than half-a-dozen miles from the Somerset border, lie the three villages of Uffculme, Culmstock and Hemyock. Each has its ancient parish church, and at one time each was an integrated community, a distinct entity fully equipped for its own needs and possessing a spirit of pride and independence. For generations there had been a considerable trade in the neighbourhood in combing and spinning wool. At one place there was a silk-factory, and at Uffculme a paper-mill had flourished until extensive

109

flooding destroyed it. Soap-making was also carried on here, the products being transported to Exeter on pack-horses. In the background is Culmstock Beacon, on which the fires of warning or rejoicing had flamed at intervals through the centuries and, when Blackmore's father came to Culmstock, as recently as twenty years before his coming, for the victory of Waterloo. A description of the neighbourhood by a resident (quoted in *The Blackmore Country* by F. J. Snell) gives a fair idea of characteristics which have survived the loss of independent local life and colour:

> "The narrowness of the lanes around adds greatly to the country's charms, their high hedgerows being a mass of many kinds of flowers. Thoroughly to enjoy the beauties of the neighbourhood, however, it must be viewed from one of the hills or downs. Embowered in a wealth of greenery, Uffculme sleeps on a slope of the Culm Valley. As far as the eye can reach, lies a most beautiful panorama of diversified hill and dale with rounded trees, every field hedged with them. The quiet herds of Devon cattle lie ruminating and adorning the green bosom of the country. The whole scene has a charming cultured aspect, as if some giant landscape-gardener had laid it out."

Looking back upon Culmstock across the span of nearly sixty years, Blackmore was inspired to write *Perlycross*, perhaps his finest work after *Lorna Doone*, and certainly one of the best pastoral novels in our language. Once again he teased the critics and the guide-

book makers with a good measure of topographical
liberty mixed with the drawing of characters based upon
the remembrance of actual persons; "Perlycross" is
Culmstock, and "Pumpington" is recognisably Wellington, but some fine estates are removed by Blackmore
many miles from their real situation. The plot, hinging
upon the disappearance of the body of Sir Thomas
Waldron from a vault beneath the church and a false
accusation of body-snatching against the local doctor,
is no stronger than most of the slender, and sometimes
threadbare, plots in Blackmore's other novels. Remarkably enough, there is scarcely any love-interest worth
mentioning, reflecting perhaps the decline of the heroine
which had been taking place in the literary world over
the past three decades.

But with all this, *Perlycross* is so clever and so obser-
vant a study of a little community that it reflects Blackmore at the height of his powers. In Sergeant Jakes (the
village schoolmaster), old Clerk Channing, and Parson
Penniloe (modelled on his own father), Blackmore has
created characters perhaps more real than any others in
his books; he was, in any case, always more successful
in this way with his men than with his women. The
character-drawing in *Perlycross* was praised by no less
a critic than George Saintsbury, and the whole vigorous
gallery of persons in the novel not unexpectedly involved
the author in many denials as to the originals con-
fidently "discovered." With a good dénouement and a
fair absence of those digressions which the reviewers had
so often deplored in his earlier works, *Perlycross* succeeds

in presenting us with a small world in which the adventures of simple people contribute to the general impression of peace, inward and outward, that reigned in this corner of the West country in the third decade of the nineteenth century. Local legends and customs are skilfully interwoven in the narrative. One of the best chapters in the book describes the great and protracted wrestling-match at the village revels between the champions of Devon and Cornwall, culminating in the collapse of the tent on top of contestants and spectators alike, who were jumbled up together "with mouths full of tallow, sawdust, pitch, and another fellow's toes." The district had known many such combats, and was to see others of even sterner nature, for Tom Sayers, the last and one of the greatest of the old bare-knuckle prizefighters, lived in this neighbourhood and fought many a fight for a three-and-sixpenny tea-service.

Blackmore's skill in describing the countryside is particularly noticeable in *Perlycross*. Consider, for example, this introduction to a desolate area around Dunkeswell, to which he gives the name "Blackmarsh":

"A long way back among the Blackdown hills, and in nobody knows what parish, the land breaks off into a barren stretch, uncouth, dark, and desolate. Being neither hill nor valley, slope nor plain, morass nor woodland, it has no lesson for the wanderer, except that the sooner he gets out of it the better. For there is nothing to gratify him if he be an artist, nothing to interest him if his tastes are antiquarian, nothing to arouse his ardour, even though

112

he were that happy and most ardent creature, a naturalist free from rheumatism. And as for any honest fellow mainly concerned with bread and butter, his head will at once go round with fear and with looking over his shoulders. For it is a lonesome and gruesome place, where the weather makes no difference; where Nature has not put her hand, on this part or on that, to leave a mark or show a preference, but slurred the whole with one black frown of desolate monotony.

That being so, the few and simple dwellers on the moorland around, or in the lowland homesteads, might well be trusted to keep their distance from this dreary solitude. There were tales enough of hapless travellers last seen going in this direction, and never in any other; as well as of spectral forms, low groans, and nightly processions through the air."

Blackmore's description is as evocative as Thomas Hardy's of Egdon Heath in *The Return of the Native*. Comparison with Hardy is inevitable; for Blackmore has in *Perlycross* done for the Culm Valley what Hardy did for Stinsford in *Under the Greenwood Tree*. "How admirable are Blackmore and Hardy!" wrote Gerald Manley Hopkins in a letter to Robert Bridges (October 1886). "But these writers only rise to their great strokes; they do not write continuously well." This true judgment could be applied to every other major English novelist; but one must point to *Perlycross* as representing a peak, inferior only to *Lorna Doone*, in its author's range of achievement. There were many others besides George Saintsbury who could appreciate its quiet qualities in

H

a year in which the circulating-library subscribers were enthusing over Du Maurier's *Trilby* and Stanley Weyman's *Under the Red Robe,* and demanding more and more of Sherlock Holmes.

X

Less than a year after the appearance of *Perlycross*
came a volume of poems by Blackmore, entitled
Fringilla. Both the American and English editions
occasioned him a good deal of annoyance. He com-
plained bitterly about his "highly finished rhythm" (although he did not, in fact, think much of himself as a
poet) being broken up into prose lines ("splatterdash")
in the former, and thought the illustrations in both cases
crude and inadequate. The book contained two long
tales in verse, and miscellaneous lyrics, some of them,
on an eighteenth-century pattern, possibly influenced by
Austin Dobson. The most notable poem in the book is
entitled "To Fame," and merits quotation here as truly
reflecting its author's sentiments about earthly laurels
and his serene acceptance of the transitoriness of the
treasure that is not of the heart :

I

Bright Fairy of the morn, with flowers arrayed,
   Whose beauties to thy young pursuer seem
   Beyond the ecstasy of poet's dream—
Shall I o'ertake thee, ere thy lustre fade?

II

Ripe glory of the noon, august, and proud,
   A vision of high purpose, power, and skill,
   That melteth into mirage of good-will—
Do I o'ertake thee, or embrace a cloud?

115

THE LAST VICTORIAN

III

Gray shadow of the evening, gaunt and bare,
  At random cast, beyond me or above,
  And cold as memory in the arms of love—
If I o'ertook thee now, what should I care?

IV

"No morn or noon, or eve am I," she said;
  But night—the depth of night behind the sun :
  By all mankind pursued; but never won,
Until my shadow falls upon a shade."

Meanwhile the light of fame was shining with ever-increasing brightness upon *Lorna Doone,* and in the early part of 1896 several national newspapers carried exciting news for the book's enormous circle of admirers :

"It has been the fashion among readers and critics for too long, to set aside any new novel by Mr. R. D. Blackmore with the half-contemptuous, half-regretful question—When shall we have another *Lorna Doone*? We are certain indeed, that hundreds and hundreds of people have missed the rare pleasure of reading some of the best and raciest romances in the language . . . take as examples *The Maid of Sker* and *Christowell* . . . simply because of the popularity of this idea. How absurd it is only the true admirers of Mr. Blackmore know. Whether or not the author has permitted himself to be troubled by this gravel-blind treatment we cannot say definitely : but at any rate he is now offering carpers the book they have been clamouring for. *Slain by the Doones: a Record of Exmoor,* will appear later in the year."

116

R. D. BLACKMORE AND HIS NOVELS

The book, published in England under the title of *Tales from the Telling House,* and in America as *Slain by the Doones,* consisted of four short stories and a Preface. The first story alone gave Blackmore's readers the background and the characters they "had been clamouring for," and little enough of either. Here Blackmore made use of one of the reputed exploits of the Doones, when they were said to have attacked and murdered a Squire who lived in a lonely part of Exmoor Forest called "The Warren." In Blackmore's account the Squire is done to death by the Doones when they come upon him fishing in a stream which they claim for their own. Later, the outlaws break into the house where Sylvia, the Squire's daughter and the narrator of the story, is living with two faithful retainers, and although the girl tries to defend herself with her father's sword, they carry her away, bound to a horse.

> "Then, when my heart was quite gone in despair, and all trouble shrank into a trifle, I heard a loud shout, and the trample of feet, and the rattle of arms, and the clash of horses. Contriving to twist myself a little, I saw that the band of Doones were mounting a saddle-backed bridge in a deep wooded glen, with a roaring water under them. On the crown of the bridge a vast man stood, such as I had never descried before, bearing no armour that I could see, but wearing a farmer's hat, and raising a staff like the stem of a young oak tree. He was striking at no one, but playing with his staff, as if it were a willow in the morning breeze.
> 'Down with him! Ride him down! Send a bullet

117

through him!' several of the Doones called out, but no one showed any hurry to do it. It seemed as if they knew him, and feared his mighty strength, and their guns were now slung behind their backs on account of the roughness of the way."

A desperate charge at the vast man by Charlie Doone proves in vain, and the rider's sword is dashed from his grasp:

"'Now for another!' the farmer cried, and his deep voice rang above the roar of Lynn; 'or two at once, if it suits you better. I will teach you to carry off women, you dogs!'"

This is the only glimpse we have of John Ridd, Lorna does not appear at all, and the brief showing of Carver Doone adds nothing to what we already know about his villainy and his "horrible visage." Blackmore, yielding to the pressure of his public and his publisher, probably wrote the story with a renewed feeling of annoyance that in general estimation he was bound hand-and-foot as a literary artist to his Romance of Exmoor. In truth, he gave his expectant admirers very little in the way of a second helping; and the title of the book could not have helped to stimulate sales. The ordinary public could scarcely be expected to know that the "Telling House" denoted the place in which lost sheep, when found and brought thither, were sorted out and attached to their rightful owners.

Some compensation, however, for the disappointing

Doone episode should have been found by Blackmore's readers in the dramatic story of *George Bowring*. Set in North Wales, it tells of a student friendship carried on in after years until brought to a tragic conclusion when the narrator's friend was murdered in a remote spot near Cader Idris. He was murdered on account of his possession of a gold watch, the latter being coveted because of a superstition in those parts that "even Death must listen to the voice of Time in gold; that, when the scanty numbered moments of the sick are fleeting, a gold watch laid in the wasted palm, and pointing the earthly hours, compels the scythe of Death to pause, the timeless power to bow before the two great gods of the human race —time and gold." The strange tale witnesses to Blackmore's strong sense of the numinous and his sympathetic understanding of those in whom, through ignorance, superstition has to serve for faith. In *Crocker's Hole* Blackmore makes use of a Culm legend, and reveals his intimate knowledge of angling, but the whole is little more than an incident retailed with a rather strained attempt at humour. *Frida; or the Lover's Leap* is based on a legend of the coast near Lynton; for many years the story had circulated that one Jennifred de Wichehalse, being deserted by her lover, Lord Auberley, in the days of James II, had flung herself over the cliffs at Duty Point. Researches carried out in the early years of this century have shown the story to be false; and the basis for it can be seen in the fact that the last survivor of the unfortunate Wichehalse family, named Mary, being deprived of her inheritance by her father's finan-

119

cial extravagance, spent much of her time wandering along the coast in melancholy loneliness and at the end mysteriously disappeared.

These four tales provide interest and good examples of Blackmore's craft for those who will be ready to find such pleasures outside the pages of *Lorna Doone*. In this volume the novelist could very fittingly have taken leave of his readers, and been gratefully remembered in this last excursion to fields he had made so much his own. The pity was that only a few months after the book had appeared he was struggling with the composition of his final novel, which by style and manner was doomed even before it had started on its fruitless rounds of the American magazines.

As the century drew to its close, Blackmore's life faded with it. On top of his arthritis, he suffered from intestinal disorder, which caused him much sleeplessness and the necessity to use some drugs for this complaint. "My memory," he wrote to Mrs. Alfred Hunt in April, 1897, "gets blurred and cracked . . . and my walks now are of the lame duck order." However, the occasion of the Diamond Jubilee in this year, celebrating so much of what he had always regarded as true achievement and virtue, stimulated him to produce a patriotic poem, "Carmen Britannicum," which was printed in "The Publishers' Circular." At the same time he went on doggedly, with many set-backs due to illness and his recognition that wholesale revising and cutting was necessary in the first draft, with his last novel. Having appeared in serial form in "Blackwood's Magazine," it

was published in one volume, with drawings by Chris
Hammond, towards the close of 1897.

Dariel is sub-titled "A romance of Surrey," but the locality is not precisely indicated; the situation of Crogate
Hall, the narrator's home, seems to have been somewhere
in the neighbourhood of Leatherhead, perhaps not far
from the old farm of Meredith's *Diana of the Crossways*.
Occasionally in the descriptive writing where Surrey is
concerned, there is a flash of the old skill, but the plot,
making use of the vendetta motive which was prominent
in *Clara Vaughan,* is tediously involved, and the characters bear little resemblance to human beings. The hand
that moved the puppets in this last work was plainly one
that was very tired. When, at the end of the story, the
ample ghost of John Ridd turns up in the Caucasus to
save the day and rout the loathsome ruffians, it is difficult to believe that it is the same pen which so graphic-
ally described the battles between virtue and lawlessness
on Exmoor that is now trying vainly to give reality to a
pasteboard contest in a sham moonlight.

In a notice of *Cripps the Carrier* in "The Academy,"
the reviewer, having remarked that "Mr. Blackmore is
capable of high art," had gone on "to ask that his next
book shall have a broader area and theme than a love-
story in a corner of Oxfordshire." This criticism was
singularly wide of the mark, for it was always when
dealing with a rural "corner" of England that Blackmore's best work was done. When he strayed abroad in
his writings, handicapped as he was by his own com-
plete lack of experience as a traveller and by the pre-

valent conception of "foreigners" as mostly dishonest and treacherous, he achieved little of value and was rarely able, in fact, to rise much above melodrama. In *Lorna Doone, Perlycross, Christowell,* and *Cripps the Carrier,* Blackmore mercifully made no expeditions overseas, but established a claim by these books to be, after Thomas Hardy, our finest exponent of the pastoral novel. It may be that as the time and manners they depict recede still further from us, and our unfulfilled longing for what was best in that far away simplicity increases as our rural regions are gradually engulfed, we shall rediscover some of these books and be grateful for them, as we are grateful for Hardy himself, and for Quiller-Couch and Walter Raymond and William Barnes.

The poor reception of *Dariel* brought added pain to Blackmore in the fact that a reviewer in "The Academy" had accused the author of achieving in one chapter "a triumph of vulgarity." Remembering what is the usual conception in the mind of the average reader of fiction, of being "vulgar", it was ironical indeed that such an adjective should have been applied to so sturdy a defender of the strict proprieties. The chapter thus labelled contains some stilted dialogue and equally stilted love-making between Grace Cranleigh and one Jackson Stoneman, a stockbroker, in a dairy, and is never for one moment lively or real enough to warrant any description save that of extreme and somewhat nauseating sentimentality. Even though he chose the wrong word, it is difficult not to feel some sympathy with a reviewer who met this kind of thing and found it impossible not to complain :

> "To reassure herself, she whispered something altogether repugnant to the spirit of the Stock Exchange, silver and gold, and even jewels. But that blessed stockbroker knew the quickest way to close transactions. He swept back a mint-worth of ductile gold from the sapphires whose lustre was tremulous with dew, and he gazed at them gently, tenderly, triumphantly, yet not without fear and diffidence. 'All this committed to my charge?' he asked, with the other arm defining the flexuous circuit of his future realm.
> 'It may be a very poor investment,' answered Grace; 'but one thing is certain—what little there is, is entirely a genuine article.' "

And at the close, of course, there is the happy ending. Blackmore was old and ailing and lonely, but neither his own deep faith nor such readers as were prepared to look at anything of his besides *Lorna Doone* must be denied the satisfaction of the dawn after darkness, the haven after storms :

> "I led his beautiful daughter back to Sir Imar, and I said—'You see.'
> 'Yes, I see," he answered softly. 'And there is no more to be said.' "

The last chapter, covering nearly three years of intermittent pain and feebleness of limb, with the pen inactive except for occasional short letters to his friends,

123

has its moments of glory in Blackmore's undaunted sense of humour and the courage which he bore his lonely burden. Even his treasured orchards failed at the last to provide the abundant harvest which would have set a seal on the work to which he had given so much of his life. On September 27th, 1899, he wrote to Mrs. Hunt:

> "I am delighted to hear of your improved health, and hope it may still improve. For me there is no such chance, with this stubborn, internal, plague which wears me out, though slowly, and takes all good out of me. We do want rain, and all things languish, and the fruit crop is miserable."

At the end of that year Blackmore was invited to add Noel Coward to his large collection of godchildren, the future playwright having been born at Teddington to parents who were very friendly with Blackmore and whom he sometimes visited. Ten members of the Coward family sang in the choir of the "Marinette and Popinjay" church of St. Albans, to the extension of which Blackmore had refused to subscribe. He also declined, in this case, the request to act as a godfather, feeling that as so many of his godchildren had died in infancy he might be thought to have some unconscious influence of the wrong sort! In his autobiography Coward does not mention his distinguished neighbour, and of his baptism in that stately building he merely records that he "was carried to the church, damped, and carried back home, preserving throughout an attitude of serene resignation."

R. D. BLACKMORE AND HIS NOVELS

Blackmore passed away quietly on January 20th, 1900. On that very day the City Imperial Volunteers were marching through the cheering throngs of London on their way to the South African War; England had stepped proudly into the brief glories of the Victorian afterglow. The obituary notice in "The Times," giving half-a-column to Blackmore, but four-and-a-half columns to John Ruskin, who died at Coniston on the same day, stated somewhat inaccurately, in praising *Lorna Doone*, that "its merits were seen and appreciated at once." "His death," said the article, "removes a man of remarkable character—a strong, hard-working, modest, typical Englishman—and a writer distinguished by many very pleasant qualities, whose name will be kept alive by his masterpiece—the ever-delightful *Lorna Doone*."

In other columns of that issue one finds an advertisement for "A Circus Unparalleled in London" at the Crystal Palace, with 2,500 seats at sixpence each. There is also the announcement of a new novel, *Love and Mr. Lewisham*, by a thought-provoking and rising novelist named H. G. Wells.

Gomer House has gone, but a little villa among the rows of villas built on those once fertile and lovely acres, calls itself Lorna Doone, and over the back entrances one can catch glimpses of a few surviving fruit-trees from the orchards in which a great Englishman and a great writer once mused and laboured.

125